They Called Us Savages

A Hereditary Chief's Quest for Truth and Harmony

Dominique Rankin
&
Marie-Josée Tardif

Translated by Ben Vrignon

They Called Us Savages: A Hereditary Chief's Quest for Truth and Harmony

ISBN: 978-1-989282-93-9

The publisher gratefully acknowledges the support of the Canada Council for the Arts and the Manitoba Arts Council for its publishing program. We acknowledge the support of the Government of Canada through the Canada Book Fund and the Government of Manitoba through the Publishing Tax Credit Program for our publishing activities.

We acknowledge the financial support of the Government of Canada, through the National Translation Program for Book Publishing, for our translation activities.

Financé par le gouvernement du Canada
Funded by the Government of Canada

Library and Archives Canada Cataloguing in Publication

Title: They called us Savages : a Hereditary Chief's quest for truth and harmony / Dominique Rankin and Marie-Josée Tardif.
Other titles: On nous appelait les Sauvages. English
Names: Rankin, Dominique, 1947- author. | Tardif, Marie-Josée, 1967- author. | Vrignon, Ben, translator.
Description: Translation of: On nous appelait les Sauvages: souvenirs et espoirs d'un chef héréditaire algonquin.
Identifiers: Canadiana (print) 20200218778 | Canadiana (ebook) 20200218816 | ISBN 9781989282939 (softcover) | ISBN 9781989282946 (PDF) | ISBN 9781989282953 (EPUB) | ISBN 9781989282960 (Kindle)
Subjects: LCSH: Rankin, Dominique, 1947- | LCSH: Indigenous peoples—Québec (Province)—Social life and customs—20th century. | LCSH: Indigenous peoples—Québec (Province)—Biography. | CSH: Native peoples—Canada—Residential schools. | LCGFT: Autobiographies.
Classification: LCC E99.A35 R3613 2020 | DDC 971.4004/9733—dc23

English translation: Ben Vrignon
Design and layout: Relish New Brand Experience
Cover photo: Nancy Lessard
Back cover photos: Jean-Sébastien Veilleux
Editor-in-Chief: Joanne Therrien
Copy Editor: Lynne Therrien

Vidacom Publications
P.O. Box 123 Winnipeg, Manitoba Canada R2H 3B4
Tel: 204 235 0078 • admin@plaines.mb.ca • www.vidacom.ca

For my son Mak8a, Stéphane

For my daughter Sakapon, Geneviève

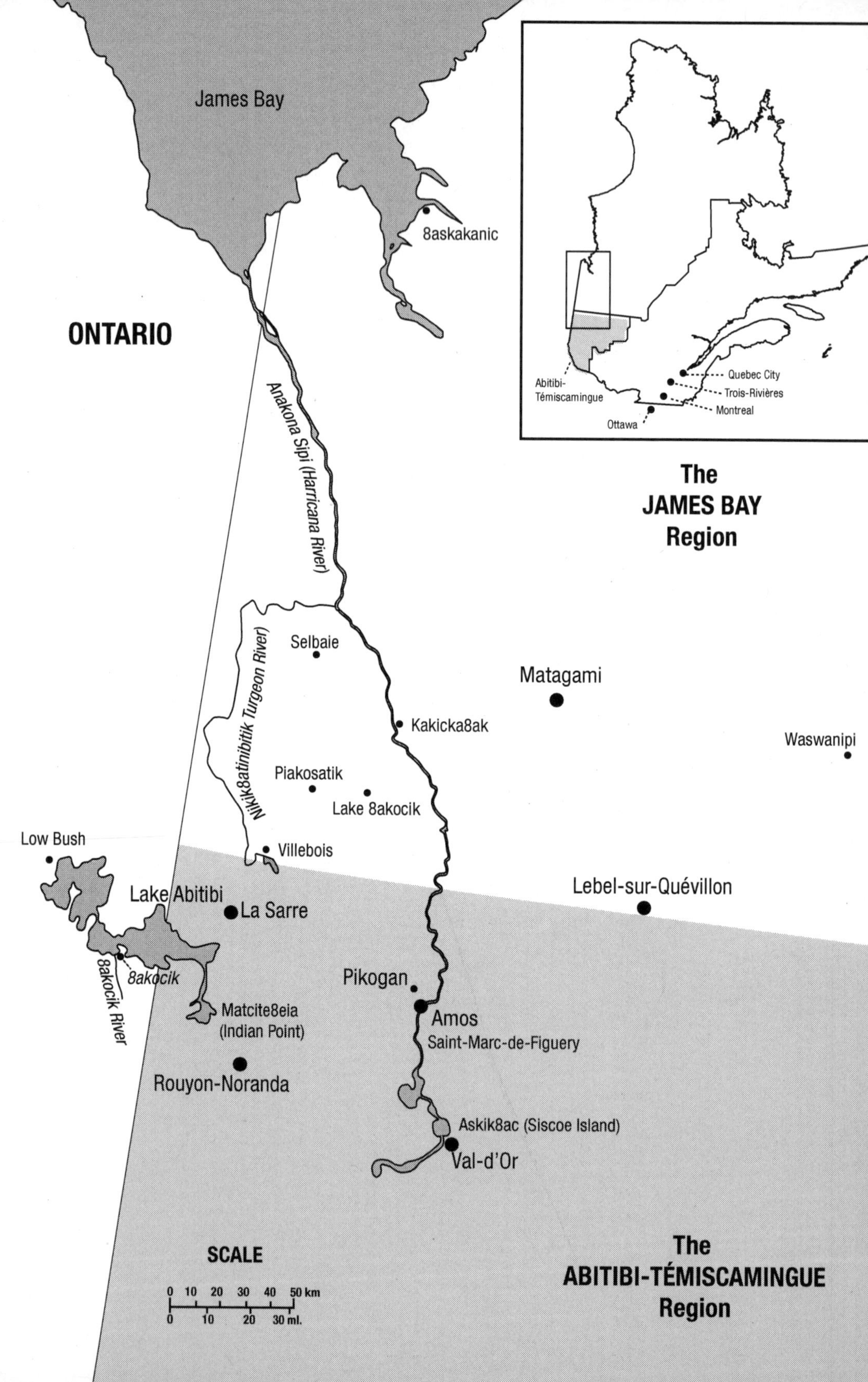
James Bay
8askakanic
ONTARIO
Anakona Sipi (Harricana River)
Abitibi-
Témiscamingue
Quebec City
Trois-Rivières
Montreal
Ottawa
The
JAMES BAY
Region
Nikik8atinibitik Turgeon River)
Selbaie
Matagami
Kakicka8ak
Waswanipi
Piakosatik
Lake 8akocik
Low Bush
Villebois
Lake Abitibi
La Sarre
Lebel-sur-Quévillon
8akocik
8akocik River
Pikogan
Matcite8eia
(Indian Point)
Amos
Saint-Marc-de-Figuery
Rouyon-Noranda
Askik8ac (Siscoe Island)
Val-d'Or
SCALE
0 10 20 30 40 50 km
0 10 20 30 ml.
The
ABITIBI-TÉMISCAMINGUE
Region

A Note on the Algonquin Alphabet

Originally, the Algonquin language did not have its own writing system. European missionaries gave it a written form, based on a syllabic alphabet. At the time, the letter "w" did not exist in the French alphabet, and as a result, the missionaries of New France chose to employ "***8***" (the ligature "*ou*") to represent a "w" sound, as in *Washington* or *water.* In practice, however, "***8***" was often substituted for the glyph "8." According to Algonquin pronunciation, the letter "t" is also sometimes pronounced as a "d." And so, the given name "Dominique" is rendered "T8aminik" in Algonquin. In this case, the "8" simply stretches the following "a."

Here is a simplified pronunciation guide for the Algonquin alphabet:

Vowels: a, e, i, o
Consonants: p, c, t, k, n, s, 8, m, tc

Letters	Pronunciation
a	ah
c	sh or j (as in *Jacques* or *Taj Mahal*)
e	short **e** (as in *bed*)
i	ee
k	k or hard **g** (as in *guardian*)
m	m
n	n
o	**o** or **oo** (as in *food*)
p	p or b
s	s or z
t	t or d
tc	tch
8	w

Foreword

More than ever, at ninety-seven years old, I must live the life Creator gives me day to day! I am nevertheless preparing to pass on the torch to the representatives of the younger generations, and among them, to my spiritual son, T8aminik Rankin.

Over the years, T8aminik managed to overcome numerous obstacles that Indigenous Peoples have had to face. One of these obstacles, and by no means the least surmountable, was for them to be perceived as "Savages."

I held T8aminik in my arms when he was but a small child and we shared many ceremonies in the company of his father, my best friend. And, over the last twenty years, I accompanied him closely on the path of Traditional Medicine. Among all the teachings I passed on to him, one of my favourite topics was that of the Wampum Belt that describes the Prophecy of the Seven Fires.

In 1970, I became the guardian of three Wampum Belts, including the Seven Fires Belt. These Sacred Medicine Items were once protected by Pakina8atik, my great-grandfather's father. The Prophecy of the Seven Fires has been at the heart of my ancestors' Oral Tradition for hundreds of years,[i] but it is equally well known among other Indigenous Nations, such as the Otcip8e.[ii]

T8aminik's personal story, like the stories of all Indigenous people, is mysteriously inscribed in this prophecy. His healing came to pass at the bitter end of a long period of systematic and blatant oppression

i The Prophecy itself may be older, but many believe the Seven Fires Wampum Belt to be at least six hundred years old.

ii Pronounced "O-djib-way."

(the Indian residential school system is but one of its dark chapters), which had a direct impact on him, his family, and his community. Throughout the years, T8aminik has shared the powerful emotions he experienced on his path to healing with innumerable individuals, Indigenous and non-Indigenous alike, here and abroad.

I have also witnessed the inexhaustible energy he has dedicated to securing Indigenous Peoples in North America the worldwide recognition they deserve. Being perfectly fluent in the Algonquin and Cree languages, and possessing a firm handle on French and English, T8aminik has increasingly focused on intercultural and interfaith projects, and on defending culture and peace. His knowledge and experience impart a unique perspective to these varied projects, whether they take place in this country or elsewhere.

His ceremonies and his Sacred Pipes (one of which was entrusted to him by me) have guided and supported thousands of individuals. They have inspired us, and incited us to respect and honour our Mother Earth and all of Creation. His work has paved the way for the celebration of Indigenous spirituality and cultural heritage, all while guaranteeing the inclusion of our traditions in historical accounts that concern the Anicinape.

I believe many of you will be inspired by his life, his example, and his teachings. I also believe that you will be touched by the message of the Seven Fires, for it concerns all of Earth's inhabitants in this vital time when they are called upon to make crucial choices, both in their personal and community lives.

Mik8etc to T8aminik for keeping the spirit of our ancestors alive for the benefit of our future generations.[i]

William Commanda
Algonquin Elder
Founder of the Circle of All Nations
July 2011

i Grandfather William Commanda drafted this foreword a month before leaving us for the Spirit World, mere days before the first edition of this book went to print. He passed away in his sleep at dawn on August 3, 2011. He was ninety-seven years old. *Kitci mik8etc, Comis!* Thank you so much, Grandfather!

A Word from Marie-Josée Tardif

I reflected a long time on the style of writing best suited for this work. If you are lucky enough to one day meet T8aminik Rankin, you will at once note that neither French (the language this book was originally published in) nor English are his mother tongue. Nonetheless, T8aminik is fluent in seven languages and dialects—Algonquin (Mami8inni dialect), Cree, Otcip8e, Atikamekw, Innu, French, and English, listed here in descending order of proficiency. Still, T8aminik typically formulates his thoughts in Algonquin before translating them into a language other than his own. As direct translations are not always possible, inherent difficulties arise from this, which, combined with the variety of French and English he learned in Quebec, his colourful sense of humour, and his unique storytelling talent, confers to his spoken language an unconventional, incomparable flavour.

Had I opted to fastidiously transcribe T8aminik's distinctive manner of speech, the original French manuscript of this book (first published in 2011) would have been virtually indecipherable to most readers. I therefore chose to pen his account in a more literary style, allowing the words to flow freely in my first language, while remaining as close as possible to the spirit of his narration, ideas, and fundamental message. This English edition of *On nous appelait les Sauvages* endeavours to do the same, and was prepared under the scrutiny of both T8aminik and myself. Since I have had the opportunity to study Traditional Medicine and the Mami8inni dialect by T8aminik's side, I hope, with no little humility, to count among those who have managed to faithfully translate some of what Indigenous Peoples have been attempting to convey to their non-Indigenous brothers and sisters for centuries.

That said, this book is for Indigenous and non-Indigenous audiences alike. In these pages, T8aminik and I hope to share an Indigenous perspective of Canadian history, and, especially, to deliver a message of hope to those who suffer from their pasts, either individually or collectively, irrespective of their ethnic backgrounds.

What you are about to read is a true account. Only a few names have been obscured or modified to protect the identities of the parties concerned. From the outset, T8aminik and I decided to pattern these memoirs on the narrative conveyed by the Prophecy of the Seven Fires. Every morning at sunrise, we would sit by a window overlooking our magnificent Laurentian Forest, and over coffee, I would interview him on the topics and themes I intended on tackling that day. Come evening, I would read him my new pages. T8aminik would then correct any Mami8inni spelling errors, clear up any inaccuracies, and enrich the text with new ideas as inspiration came to him. In essence, although this work may feature a more elaborate vocabulary than T8aminik would typically employ in French or in English, the ideas, images, and teachings expressed herein are quite his own, as well as those of his ancestors.

Like many Québécois of French-Canadian origin, my heritage is *métissé*, as some of my French ancestors intermarried with Algonquins and Mi'kmaqs. I am proud to say that one of my Acadian foremothers dared marry a First Nations man sometime in the seventeenth century, which was extremely rare for a woman of that era. Usually, mixed marriages took place between white men and Indigenous women. In New France, these unions had a two-fold goal that was perceived as a noble one at the time—to convert "Indians" to Catholicism, and to ensure population growth in the colony. However, during the Victorian era, marrying a "*Sauvage*" or "*Sauvagesse*"—an "Indian"—became increasingly taboo in Québécois society. Consequently, many of our ancestors found themselves concealing their Indigenous heritage, or disavowing it outright. At long last, our generation has begun breaking the silence that once reigned, and has slowly been reopening the floodgates to this rich and long-neglected legacy.

It is perhaps owing to the white and red blood that runs through my veins that I genuinely love establishing bridges between humans. Indeed, I am filled with a profound sense of satisfaction as I write these lines. Nonetheless, I know that the very first bridge to build will have to address the contradictions, the paradoxes, and the ruptures that exist in each and every one of us.

Marie-Josée Tardif (Oteimin Kokom)

Prologue

For three days and three nights now, I've been perched on this wretched platform where I must fast. *Pitapan*—sunrise—is about to pierce the horizon. I barely slept a wink last night, and when I finally managed to drift off into slumber, my dreams were flooded with images of chicken dishes, sardines, and large bowls of *8apos-8apo*, the succulent hare soup that Mom loved making when we were children. It'll soon be the fourth dawn of this trial, during which for twenty-one days, I must remain on a platform of about nine square metres, nested atop an immense hundred-year-old pine tree, without food or drink.

I mechanically stuff my Sacred Pipe for the short Sunrise Ceremony. I pray, but despite myself, my thoughts wander back to my unease: "Why all these dreams of food? After all, it isn't my first time fasting . . ." In fact, it's been at least a week since I last ate. I spent many days preparing my body and soul for this final trial, the test that will allow my entry into the Circle of Elders. My internal lamentations persist: "It's the thirst that's giving me a hard time," I tell myself. "On top of that, I have to stand the cold, the rain, and the wind. I've had it up to here with walking in circles up on this roost."

It's been fifty years since I embraced my vocation as a Medicine Man. Five decades of learning, of renunciation, of ceremonies, of initiations all across the country, but this time, I'm pretty sure that my teachers have pushed me to my limits. I admit it, I'm ready to give up. This morning, I find that I'm no longer impressed by this powerful place, where who knows how many Medicine Men have fasted before me. The forest's beauty has now been erased from my field of vision. I no longer feel protected by the feathers, animal skulls, and coloured Tobacco Ties that surround me, swaying gently from the branches of this majestic tree. In the solitude of my retreat, far away from everything—even the ground!—I give in to what truly haunts me: my past.

Weakened by hunger and physical discomfort, I'm no longer able to keep things in perspective and to push away my memories. Images and thoughts from another time persist—the games and laughter of my tender youth in the heart of the boreal forest; the multitudes of teachings I received from Elders; the long canoe trips with my family, where spectacular landscapes scrolled by before our eyes; the delight of being among wild animals; the full, busy days I spent outside, breathing in the invigorating winter air; the starry nights by the tipi in the summertime . . . And suddenly—my parents, powerless to stop the authorities from throwing me, along with my brothers and sisters, into a government-chartered bus; our arrival at the residential school for Indian children; the shock of those first moments in that insane universe, in which some supposedly well-meaning politicians and religious figures had hoped to turn us into "proper white children." I can clearly see the missionaries' faces and hear their voices as they cast us into an abyss of collective madness—a world in which the law of silence reigned supreme. For years, these black-robed men and women violated each and every facet of our beings with total impunity—our culture, our language, our beliefs, our hearts, our souls, our spirits, and even our bodies.

In spite of these overwhelming memories, my Pipe Ceremony calms me and I focus a bit. I put away my Sacred Bundle, and suddenly I hear *Comis*[i] Mikisi's booming voice from the foot of my tree: "*Ki ki mino nipa na*? Did you sleep well?" the Elder teases, climbing the wooden ladder leading to the platform. This old crease-cheeked, eagle-eyed Otcip8e is the guide I chose to see me through the initiation. Every morning, he visits me to check in on my physical—and mental—state.

Comis finds himself a spot by my side and hands me a pine cone the size of a banana. "*Minik8en mackiki.* Drink the Medicine," he orders me with kindness in his voice. As I've done from time to time over the last

---

i "Spiritual Grandfather." Pronounced "Shoo-miss."

three days, I break the cone in half and quickly suck out the fluid it contains. This high-vitamin sap will be my only nourishment for the duration of the trial. Truth be told, it soon satiates me, and I'll seldom turn to it for the rest of my sojourn atop the tree. At any rate, right now I'm finding the Elder's presence reassuring and irritating, all at once.

"You're angry," notices my guide, in a soft tone.

"Yes," I answer, barely hiding my annoyance. "I know that you've eaten this morning. I can even smell the food on your body and your clothes. You reek of *sasopok8ecikan*!"[i]

After a brief silence, the Medicine Man begins again, carefully measuring his words: "I'll be honest with you. The trial you're undergoing isn't an easy one. The next days are bound to be even more gruelling if you refuse to face what's truly bothering you. You know very well that your real obstacle is neither hunger nor thirst, but acceptance."

"I've taken part in so many rituals in the hope of accepting my past or *our* past, that I've lost count!" I reply. "I thought I'd turned the page."

"When one turns the page and believes to have moved on, a new layer of the story becomes ripe for healing. This is as true for a person as it is for a family or a nation. When our spirits are ready to do so, we can shed our skins like snakes. Only then can we begin a new chapter in our lives, freer than before. And, eventually, one fine day, we discover that the past and future no longer have any hold over us. This opens our spirit to the beauty of the now."

Comis Mikisi takes a seat behind me and, with the tips of his fingers, starts massaging my head. He's guessed—correctly—that I'm suffering from a nasty headache. He resumes the lesson:

"Never lose sight of the Seven Fires Wampum Belt. The Anicinape[ii] Prophets transmitted these teachings with the children of the future in mind, who, like you, will have known the hardships of persecution and injustice. Everything up to now has been foretold, and it looks like the coming chapters will unfold as it's been said they would. Hang in there,

i Traditional fried bread.
ii Pronounced "Ah-nee-shee-nah-bay."

my boy. You must first pass this test for the sake of future generations. You must think of them."

My guide's wise words give me something to reflect on over the next few days. He's right. Should I be surprised at what other Indigenous youths must have suffered, like me, behind the closed doors of residential schools? In truth, our peoples had long ago been warned about the dangers that would accompany the arrival of the "light-skinned race." Several centuries ago, long before the arrival of Christopher Columbus, John Cabot, and Jacques Cartier, seven Anicinape Prophets had predicted that the meeting of our two civilizations would be a pivotal moment and could lead to our undoing. It was also known that after innumerable trials, an important renaissance would emerge, which could lead to reconciliation and allow us to form a single, great family founded on sharing and respect.

The darkest night in the history of Indigenous Peoples in Canada ended with the abolition of the residential school system at the end of the last century. When I was freed from it, we were at the crossroads of the Prophecy's Fifth Fire. In order for the Sixth and Seventh Fires to come to pass, and for the good of future generations, I was ready to do my part and to continue healing.

Ickote Kitcipison

THE BEADS THAT TELL OUR STORY

I must have been around thirty when the Prophecy of the Seven Fires was revealed to me. The Wampum Belt that told of these very ancient teachings had just been entrusted to *Comis* William Commanda, my father's best friend, and the man who would later become my principal spiritual guide.

This shell bead belt was crafted in the fifteenth century, or perhaps even earlier. Yet, the Prophecy that is encoded in it is much more ancient. It has been passed down from generation to generation among the Algonquin people and the Otcip8e[i] (a sister Nation with which we share a language and a way of life) since sometime in the distant past, in an age that long predated the arrival of the first Europeans on our continent.

Once, the Seven Fires Wampum Belt had been protected by Pakina8atik, William Commanda's great-great-grandfather. The Belt should have been passed down to William through his grandfather and his father. But the object itself and the message it carries were once considered subversive by the religious authorities of Quebec. So much so that for many years, the Belt was hidden by Elders, some of whom lived very far away. In 1970, the precious Wampum Belt found its way to Kitigan Zibi, in the Maniwaki region, and Grandfather William became its official guardian. About ten years passed before he felt that the time had come for him to reveal it to the world and share its teachings with all nations.

In the mid-nineties, William Commanda met Eddie Benton-Banai, an Elder from the Lac Courtes Oreilles Otcip8e reservation in Wisconsin.

i These related peoples both identify as Anicinape *(plural: Anicinapek).*

The latter was passing through Ontario and wanted to hold a conference on the Prophecy of the Seven Fires. *Comis* William attended and was struck by the similarities between the teachings that had been passed down by his own ancestors and those of this Elder who hailed all the way from Wisconsin. After the conference, he approached Grandfather Eddie and showed him our Wampum Belt: "Is this the Belt of which you spoke?" It was the first time that Mr. Benton-Banai had come into contact with the Sacred Item—he was deeply moved. He confided to William that he had had a vision of the Seven Fires story. He had transcribed this vision, and the resulting text pleased Grandfather William to no end, for it indeed corresponded to our own Oral Tradition. From that day forward, he shared this written version of the Prophecy with anyone who wished to receive the Wampum Belt's teachings. Now, I'm very happy to be able to share it with you.

These days, a growing number of people from all nations are discovering the Prophecy of the Seven Fires, though in my language, we call it *Ickote kitcipison*. *Ickote* is the fire, while *kitcipison* designates an arrangement of shell beads assembled to depict a particular image—pearls of wisdom that hold a priceless teaching. A Wampum Belt is just that: a visual message that can symbolize and seal an alliance between peoples, or help us better understand an aspect of human nature and its challenges.

Writing doesn't exist in the Anicinape tradition. We've always favoured teaching by example, conscious of the fact that actions leave more of an impression than words do. A Wampum Belt's custodian should therefore not only be thoroughly versed in the message it contains, but should also—and most importantly—be able to understand and integrate its teachings, for this individual is responsible for ensuring that its legacy is passed on. Among all our Sacred Medicine Items, the *kitcipison* is the most important and the rarest. A keeper of a Wampum Belt has been declared by his peers worthy of protecting his Nation's most precious teachings. Hence, when you meet such a custodian, you know that you're in the presence of a most noble person. My spiritual guide, William Commanda, was the keeper of four Wampum Belts. Practically no other contemporary Medicine Man in the Americas had ever been entrusted with so much spiritual responsibility. It's an immense honour and privilege to have been one of his close students.

When William first revealed the Belt to us, my father was still alive. It was he who essentially guided me on the path of Medicine back then. In those days, *Comis* William regularly invited Elders belonging to different Nations to very private spiritual gatherings. They took place at his home in the Outaouais, on the Kitigan Zibi reserve.

That day, I accompanied my father as an apprentice. We were about twenty Medicine Men, warming our hearts by the Sacred Fire. Next to us lay tranquil Lac Bitobi, barely disturbed by the September breeze. We sat in a circle, atop a bed of freshly picked balsam fir branches on which we had laid our Sacred Items, waiting for *Comis* to tell us an extraordinary story. After a short Sacred Pipe Ceremony, William unrolled the piece of fabric that protected the Belt, and delicately held up the precious object for us to behold. Like other Wampum Belts, the shell beads that constituted the background were purple. The image itself, on the other hand, was made up of white beads. In this case, the illustration was very simple: eight diamonds aligned side by side, but the two centre ones—the fourth and fifth diamonds—overlapped to create a single symbol.

The audience was calm and attentive, and *Comis* began telling the story of the Seven Fires. Each Fire is a teaching bequeathed by a Prophet, and each of these seven Prophets had received a vision that foretold the events the Anicinape Peoples would live through over the course of their history. Thus, each Fire corresponds to an era in the future.

The Anicinape Prophets had described the blessed age when our peoples had led happy lives in perfect harmony with nature. Then, they had predicted the arrival of the light-skinned race onto our lands, and had warned us about the dangers we would encounter. Behind their smiles, these strangers could be hiding the face of death. Yet, the Prophets had also prophesied that, after a long period of suffering, our peoples could experience a renaissance, and a wave of reconciliation would spread and touch all nations.

I was impressed and intrigued all at once. How had these Elders managed to keep their teachings alive and pass them down intact? And, most of all, how had they managed to predict the future so accurately?

With Grandfather William's narrative over, the talking stick passed from hand to hand. One by one, the members of our small assembly were called upon to speak their piece.

"*Ickote kitcipison* tells of a time when our peoples lived a life that was simple, but filled with happiness," one Elder said. "*Matci Manto*—the Evil Spirit—didn't exist then. Everything was pure. My parents and grandparents used to tell me of how easy the hunt once was. Our forests were full of game. We didn't have to roam for miles and miles to find something to eat. All men were the guardians of their own territory. They knew how to manage wildlife. Meat, fish, the trees, and the plants were healthy. Humans lived long lives."

There was no condemnation or bitterness in the old Algonquin's tone, though perhaps the faintest tinge of melancholy. The stick changed hands, and another Medicine Man took the floor in a calm and composed voice.

"In those days, we weren't 'hunters.' We were *anoki8inni*—the proud men who protect and provide. We would seek out what Creator had placed on Earth so that we could live. We did not kill the animal, but asked it for its life—which is a very different thing. No one then could have imagined that one day, animals would be sold for their furs, or even less, that an entire species could be eliminated with no regard for the consequences. Where is the balance in such an outlook on life?"

When I received the talking stick, I expressed my joy at discovering this Prophecy and learning about the Fires. Back then, my healing was not yet complete. It had been twenty years since I had left the residential school, but I still vacillated between the influences of the modern age and the more stable roots of Anicinape philosophy. "My father taught me to love fire," I continued. "Fire feeds us. Fire dances and sings. When we learn to watch it and to listen to it, it inspires us and speaks to us. I like that the Prophecy speaks of fire the way it does. The missionaries taught me to fear fire. They used to show us these images of ugly demons with goatees and horns. With the end of his pitchfork, the Devil would throw humans into a great inferno—Hell—where men and women would burn for eternity. I still don't know for certain whether the Devil should be feared."

I handed the talking stick to the Elder sitting to my left, and he addressed the entire group:

"Before the Black Robes set foot in our lands, our peoples—and nature—were healthy. Today, we can no longer use cattail flour to make bread as we once did, because the ponds and the lakes are suffocating. Berries aren't what they used to be—we can no longer use them to dye our clothes. Women don't even dare wash their faces with river water . . . Don't you know who the Devil is yet? Well, then, I'll tell you. The Devil is he who has brought destruction with his knowledge and his need to dominate. We should have seen past his black robe, for too often, his heart was the same colour. It is he—the one with the afflicted heart—who has fomented evil among us."

While I absorbed these teachings, a new light was cast on my past and my origins. The books of my youth—those that told Canada's history—came back to me. The images shown to us by the missionaries back at the residential school were full of violence. They depicted First Nations scalping white explorers, suspending Jesuits above great fires, or flaying them alive. One day, I had secretly stolen a schoolbook to provoke my father during my summer vacation. "You lied to me!" I had shouted with contempt. "There are Chiefs killing white men everywhere in this book. You're a Chief. Why didn't you tell me about these crimes?"

After flipping through the book's pages one by one, my father remained silent for a long time. He didn't know how to read, but he could understand the meaning of these images depicting the "History of Canada." What we knew about our past, as it was told by our own kind, had nothing to do with all this bloodshed and these conquests. My father couldn't understand it.

Up until that fateful day when the Seven Fires Wampum Belt was revealed to me, I hadn't been sure that having been chosen to succeed my father as Hereditary Chief and Medicine Man was a good thing. I had begun making my peace with the difficult residential school ordeal and I gladly accompanied my father to ceremonies and meetings with Elders, but my future still seemed unclear.

When we conjured up the role of a Medicine Man or Woman, our people had resorted to using the term *mantoke* to designate one who worked with evil spirits. People like my father had never known such a concept. Since they had lived among Elders for a long time, their vision was not troubled, unlike the younger generations. They had a good understanding of the reach and depth of our Medicine, which only strives to stimulate or to re-establish the natural course of life in the mind and body when one or the other is off-balance. Yet, owing to evangelization, our beliefs had been considerably transformed and many among us, bit by bit, began to consider a *mantoke* to be a strange being—a "shaman" . . . a sorcerer.

For this reason, even at the age of thirty, I didn't dare speak of my legacy outside the Circle of Elders. I worried that other Anicinapek might think that I was crazy. I feared judgment. The Wampum Belt's teachings gradually gave me a new perspective. They brought me back to my true history, my culture, and my faith. The Prophecy of the Seven Fires described a time when we lived symbiotically with nature, an era that was followed by a destructive chapter for Mother Earth and humans. It revealed how humans had become mired in suffering, but also how they could make things right again. Still to this day, this Prophecy enlightens me. It helps me keep faith and inspires me to choose the best path forward. In this new era of proliferating wars and natural catastrophes, one in which the voices of Anicinapek are beginning to be heard all over the globe, I realize to what extent the Seven Fires can light the way for all nations.

Since we're currently entering a delicate phase in history, and because the message of *Ickote kitcipison* concerns all those who call Earth home, Grandfather William felt that these teachings should not only be transmitted orally, as per tradition, but also in writing. For these reasons, Grandfather encouraged me to commit my story to paper and publish this book, which I present to you with the precious help of journalist and apprentice Medicine Woman Marie-Josée Tardif, also known as Oteimin Kokom.

First Fire

ANICINAPE: THE HUMAN BEING IN HARMONY WITH NATURE

Seven major nee-gawn-na-kayg' (prophets) came to the Anishinabe. They came at a time when the people were living a full and peaceful life on the northeastern coast of North America. These prophets left the people with seven predictions of what the future would bring. Each of these prophecies was called a Fire and each Fire referred to a particular era of time that would come in the future. Thus, the teachings of the seven prophets are now called the Neesh-wa-swi' ish-ko-day-kawn' (Seven Fires) of the Ojibway.

The first prophet said to the people:

> "In the time of the First Fire, the Anishinabe nation will rise up and follow the Sacred Shell of the Midewiwin[i] Lodge. The Midewiwin Lodge will serve as a rallying point for the people and its traditional ways will be the source of great strength. The Sacred Megis[ii] will lead the way to the chosen ground of the Anishinabe. You are to look for a turtle-shaped island that is linked to the purification of the Earth. You will find such an island at the beginning and end of your journey. There will be seven stopping places along the way. You will know that the chosen ground has been reached when you come to a land where food grows on water. If you do not move, you will be destroyed."

–Edward Benton-Banai, *The Mishomis Book*

i The *Midewiwin*, or *Mitete8in*, is the body of knowledge transmitted by Anicinape Medicine Men and Women from generation to generation. These ancestral healing methods concern the body as well as the spirit.

ii *Megis*, or *Mekis*, means "shell."

When I'm asked which Nation I belong to, I answer: "I am Anicinape," a term which simply means "human being." Some translate "Anicinape" as "real man" or as "human living in harmony with nature." All these translations are correct. For us, where a human being comes from geographically is not very important. Long ago, when we came across representatives from a different Nation, we often said that we had discovered "new faces" from the East, the South, the West, or the North.

New concepts emerged when the first light-skinned people set foot on the continent. Gradually, the people of my Nation came to be identified as "Algonquins." I believe this designation derives from the 8endat[i] language, but it certainly doesn't belong to our vocabulary. All the same, we have adopted it readily and often use it to designate the Algonquian family, that is to say our greater extended family, whose members share related languages, a history, and a similar way of life. This big Algonquian family currently consists of nine Nations: Mami8inni, Otcip8e, Cree, Innu, Naskapi, Atikamekw, Abenaki, Maliseet, and Mi'kmaq.

For our part, when it comes to distinguishing our Nation from others, we have always used the term Mami8inni. It's an amusing name and we're very fond of it. It evokes our love for the berries that Mother Earth provides us during the mild season—strawberries, raspberries, blueberries, and the like. In order to pick these berries, one must bend over. And what's the first thing newcomers see when they come upon an entire community picking berries? A whole family of rear ends—small ones, big ones, meaty ones, skinny ones, young ones, old ones—pointing peacefully toward the sun! That's who we are—the tribe with rear ends proudly raised to the skies!

Whoever finds their way to our home will quickly discover that humour is one of our people's defining character traits. In fact, all Indigenous Peoples possess a remarkable sense of humour. We love to tease each other

i Pronounced "Wen-dat." The 8endat First Nation belongs to the great Iroquoian family, and is also known by the name "Huron."

and we're quite witty. Nevertheless, we're never sarcastic or mean-spirited. Our jokes are always rooted in tenderness and love.

Laughter has no doubt enabled us to survive the difficult ordeals we faced over the course of the last centuries. An individual, and even an entire community, can heal thanks to laughter. An Innu friend of mine springs to mind. It's said that one day he had botched his suicide. He had tried to hang himself with a necktie, but it ripped under his weight. The members of his community subsequently nicknamed him "*Cravate*"—or "Necktie"—and he's been known as such ever since. His brothers and sisters greet him thus as an amicable nod to the desperate day when Necktie had contemplated leaving this world. In doing so, everyone makes light of the incident, and—most important of all—they remind him through humour how happy they are that he's still among them.

The Innu, also known by the French name *Montagnais*, had established themselves northeast of the St. Lawrence River, while the area where I grew up is located approximately on the same parallel (the 50th), but much farther west. This area is called Abitibi, which means "where two waterways meet." Today, there are between 10 000 to 15 000 Algonquins living in the Abitibi and Outaouais regions. When the Europeans first arrived, we estimate that our population exceeded 30 000.[i] Our territory was much larger in area. It extended from Ottawa all the way to Quebec City along the St. Lawrence, called Kitci Sipi in my language—the Great Sacred River. When I was little, Elders used to teach us the migrations of our past. Today, it warms my heart to be able to share with my brothers and sisters—Indigenous and non-Indigenous alike—our own account of history. Even though contemporary historians are proving to be more neutral than their predecessors, their narratives continue to reflect perspectives influenced by their education. I'm moved to finally be able to give the floor to our ancestors, via their stories. Some details will remain vague, while others will be specific to the Anicinape Nation to which

i Furthermore, an estimated 7 to 10 million Indigenous persons lived in what is now North America when Jacques Cartier arrived. Four centuries later, their numbers dwindled to 250 000 in the United States and 100 000 in Canada. Nowadays, however, this trend has reversed. In the 2016 Census, 1.67 million Canadians (out of 35.15 million) identified as Indigenous.

I belong, but I believe that in terms of facts, the teachings of my ancestors will meet what modern history holds to be true.

Thanks to the Oral Tradition transmitted by our ancestors, we know that long ago, certain members of our Nation frequented the Abenaki near the Chutes-de-la-Chaudière, on the south shore of Quebec City. The Abenaki way of life, philosophy, and language were very similar to our own, so it was easy for us to live in harmony with them. Then came the 8endats, a Nation of traders hailing from the southwest (Ontario), who were much more sedentary than we were. According to our Elders, a Wampum Belt was made to formalize a pact of friendship and of territory sharing with the 8endats. Thus, the 8endats settled between Trois-Rivières and Quebec City. Their descendants live near Quebec City and still have a legendary nose for business.

As for us nomadic peoples, we carried on crisscrossing Kitci Sipi according to the rhythm of the seasons. At the time when the first white people began exploring the North American continent, Iroquois peoples from the south (now the United States) had made their way to our lands. They belonged to the Mohawk Nation, a somewhat territorial people. In their language, they called themselves Kanienkehaka, meaning "People of the Flint" or "People of the Spark." This proud Nation prized the art of war, unlike the Algonquin people who favoured peace, sharing, and dialogue. Wishing to establish themselves on the lands we had the habit of travelling through, the Iroquois attacked our people, who weren't familiar with warfare and didn't know how to defend themselves against such an enemy. Our ancestors, having suffered heavy casualties, chose to retreat north and west. Shortly after, it is said that the Iroquois, wishing to conquer more territories to the north, launched new offensives against us. This time, however, we were ready. The Algonquins had observed Iroquois war tactics well. Better prepared and determined to protect their own, they countered successfully and put an end to the Iroquois's expansion plans. The aftermath of these confrontations saw the Mohawks establish themselves on the banks of Kitci Sipi near Montreal, as a result of treaties with the white man and the implementation of new federal laws. Their descendants are still found there today. Mohawks retain their ancestors' strong temperament, but we have gradually learned to respect each other despite our differences.

❖

That said, all Indigenous Nations are united by a great migration. This incredible journey belongs to our very distant ancestral memory. As a result, we know that long ago, at a time when the Earth was covered in glaciers, some Anicinapek made their way from a place far, far away to the enormous island they called "Turtle Island"—their name for North America. During my lifetime, I have met scientists who have retraced our ancestors' steps. According to them, the various Indigenous Nations originate from Asia. Between 30 000 and 40 000 years ago, our distant ancestors from places such as Mongolia, China, and Russia slowly followed bison herds toward the northeast. Then, thanks to an ice bridge across the Bering Strait, they worked their way around the Arctic Circle and gradually settled our continent. This is why our faces resemble those of our Asian brothers, and why Indigenous Peoples from the North Pole all the way to the Tierra del Fuego archipelago share common philosophies. Nowhere else on Earth do we find such similar spiritual beliefs spread over such a vast territory.

Our Inuit brothers settled the Northern lands. They learned to survive on the tundra and in the bitter cold. Most of our brothers in the south learned to cultivate the land. Some learned to thrive in the extreme heat of tropical forests and deserts. Our brothers on the Pacific Coast (who hailed from the Pacific Islands, like Hawaii and Polynesia) remained closely linked to the spirit of the ocean. Our brothers in the vast prairies developed a close relationship with the horse. As for those of us who eventually called the Eastern forests home, we would become travelling people thanks to an extraordinary network of lakes and rivers, and to *Tciman*, our precious bark canoe.

For millennia, the people of my Nation led a peaceful and happy existence to the rhythm of the six annual seasons: *Pipon*, the time of frost, wind, snow, and powder; *Sik8an*, when the snow begins to melt;

Minokamin, when the earth is no longer hidden by the snow; *Nipin*, when nature is in full bloom; *Tak8akin*, when the leaves fall; and finally, *Pitcipipon*, when the snow reappears and the days become progressively shorter.

❖

In autumn, on our lands, there are always a few days when the coming cold relents and gives way to warmer weather. This period usually lasts about a week and is what you would call an "Indian summer." It would signal to us that the time had come to depart for our hunting and trapping grounds. Families would take advantage of the mild weather to pack their belongings, launch their canoes, and cover the few hundred kilometres that separated them from the place where they would spend their winter, spread out into small groups of around fifteen people each.

Before the great upheavals I would encounter at the age of eight, I got to taste the nomadic rhythm of life. Even though it has been many years since, I've retained vivid memories of the moments when our parents would prepare us for our departure: "You'll see, children, the landscapes are magnificent! New teachings await you there!" Their enthusiasm was contagious. We were so delighted at the prospect of this adventure that the preparations for the voyage didn't bother us one bit. My elder sisters and my mother would prepare extra rations of *panik*[i] and take care of packing. Meanwhile, my father and my elder brothers would hoist items and equipment onto the *ticipitakan*, a storage platform. These various articles—tarps, snowshoes, fishing nets, wood floats, and the like—would await our return six months later.

We were finally ready to take our places in the canoes. We could travel aboard fifteen to twenty boats, depending on the size of the family. The youngest children travelled in their parents' canoes, to which were tied others that ferried children who were a little older. The eldest siblings were autonomous and paddled on their own a short distance ahead. This gave them extra responsibilities and was a source of pride for them, as it demonstrated that they were worthy of the task.

---

i A type of bread ubiquitous in Indigenous cuisine. Pronounced "ba-nik" or "ba-nek."

I can remember that when the time came to cast off, we'd release the dogs so that they could follow us on land. Our ancestors weren't familiar with this animal way back in the day. This spirit was only introduced to us after the arrival of Europeans. Over the years, we adopted dogs as hunting companions, but also trained them to pull our sleds. Thinking back, I can still picture these magical scenes where the dogs roamed freely in the forest along the riverbanks. They would follow us, running behind until they were out of breath, and resting when they needed to. They had a hard time keeping up, as our canoes were faster, but their leaders knew the path well, and hunted along the way for food. A few days later, they'd end up reaching the encampment where we were to spend the next few months. I was always amazed and delighted to see them arrive triumphant and happy after having crossed such great distances. They were so free, and yet so loyal!

For the cold season, each group of two or three families would set up camp on a circular ancestral territory (several tens of kilometres in diameter), near a key watercourse. Within this large circle, we knew where the beavers, wolves, and bears lived. We'd observe the comings and goings of deer, moose, and caribou. Before long, we'd also catch sight of foxes, martens, and muskrats. We lived in harmony with these spirits of nature and many others, and they would give up their lives to us when needed. We knew how to manage this living pantry of ours, and, above all, we knew that we were responsible for these spirits' well-being.

Winters in the Abitibi are harsh. In January and February, temperatures can drop to thirty or forty degrees below zero at night. But inside our tent, Dad tended the fire and we slept well, bundled cozily in the hare fur sleeping bags Mom had made us. In the daytime, all of us kept busy. The women prepared food, made clothing, or checked the traplines for any small game Creator had decided to place in the snares or traps set by the men. Meanwhile, the men chopped wood and crafted snowshoes, sleds, or canoes. The responsibility of hunting big game fell to them as well. Their kills could feed the entire group for several days.

After the long winter months, the honks of Canada geese returning from distant southern lands would finally echo over the horizon once more. Everyone greeted them with great enthusiasm: "*K8e, k8e! Mino picaok!* Hello, hello! Welcome back!" (And under their breath, some might have added with a grin: "I'll welcome you onto my dinner plate, all right!") The geese's return signalled the arrival of spring, and thus, our own impending departure. The excitement was palpable as we packed our things once more and set off toward our summer rendezvous point. Several dozen families—and sometimes hundreds of them—would meet either at the mouth of a great waterway or on the shores of a lake. During the summertime, we'd allow big game and small fur-bearing animals to build up their strength and rear their young in peace. We wouldn't hunt or trap them at this time of the year. Instead, we'd turn to migrating birds, their eggs, fish, and berries for subsistence.

My ancestors had the habit of gathering on the shores of the great Lake Abitibi in the summer, at a location we called Matcite8eia—known as Pointe-aux-Sauvages and later Pointe-aux-Indiens (Indian Point) to white people. We knew that our people had frequented this very sacred place for quite some time. Recent scientific discoveries have confirmed its great age. In the 1990s, I developed an initiative to protect this site and its historical importance. This enabled us to secure funds to conduct archaeological digs. Researchers found a variety of artifacts such as bones, arrowheads, knives, and pipe fragments, some of which date back to at least eight thousand years.

Our Oral Tradition also speaks of an island we call Askik8ac, located about 200 kilometres east of Lake Abitibi. My father used to say that long ago, the gatherings there did not only count Mami8inni families, but faces from a number of Nations that hailed from every point of the compass. We know that our ancestors had been meeting there since time immemorial, because in our language, Askik8ac means "the place where seals meet." However, it's been quite some time since seals could have frequented the area, because today, the nearest sea is hundreds of kilometres to the north.

Askik8ac is known as "île Siscoe" (Siscoe Island) to white people, and is an island on Lac Kienawisik, in the Val-d'Or region. A few decades ago, Anicinapek were forced to abandon Askik8ac forever, when the island was acquired by a mining company and the Royal Canadian Mounted Police ordered First Nations populations to vacate the grounds.

In the spring, we moved around on frozen lakes and rivers even as the snow began to melt. Our ancestors taught us how to estimate the thickness of the ice by its hue, and this enables us to assess whether the path is safe or not. Drownings are rare among our people, because those who have learned to observe nature well do not push their luck and try to test it. An Anicinape will never take his canoe out if the waves are too rough. Neither will he go out in bad weather. Rain, storms, and blizzards are times for rest. We stay dry inside our homes and take the opportunity to meditate, to chat, or to craft beautiful objects. After all, animals live by the same wisdom. In bad weather, they opt to stay warm in their nests or their dens.

Much like many bird species, we knew how to choose the opportune moment to start our great biannual migration. The Elders could forecast the weather by paying close attention to the messages nature provided, were it the direction of the winds, the colour of a sunset, or how clouds appeared in the moonlight. We wore snowshoes for the spring journey. Women carried their babies in *tikinakans*,[i] while men and older children hauled the baggage-laden sleds. The journey took several days, but there was no need to hurry, for it was a pleasure, not a chore. When we felt weary, we simply stopped and set up camp for the night.

---

i Dorsal baby carriers. The well-swaddled baby is slipped into a fur-lined leather envelope tied to a wooden frame. A half-hoop is fastened to the frame's upper structure to protect the child in the event that the *tikinakan* falls. This ingenious baby carrier also floats. Thanks to the forward-facing half-hoop, the *tikinakan* rights itself automatically in case of an accident, and the baby floats safely on its back until it can be retrieved.

Happy reunions awaited those who reached our destination. The first ones on site would take bets on whose silhouettes were creeping over the horizon. After the long, cold winter months spent away from others, this was a time for celebrating. Days filled with warmth and sunshine were returning at last, and we made good use of them by holding various ceremonies and sharing the latest news. Upon arriving, each family took up its usual spot. Having left the tipi poles behind the previous year, all it took was to wrap them once more with big game furs. Setting up our shelters took no more than thirty minutes.

Then, the Medicine Men and Women would set up the *Matato* and the *Kosapacikan*—the Sweat Lodge and the Shaking Tent used for healing rituals. Medicine Men and Women from Algonquian Nations have passed down the *Mitete8in* teachings since the dawn of time. This Traditional Knowledge is transmitted orally or via the Sacred *Mekis* (shell), that is to say, the Wampum Belts. The *Mitete8in* represents a body of knowledge that empowers humans to live a healthy life in their bodies, hearts, and spirits. Anicinape Medicine Men and Women therefore know how to heal with plants and other natural remedies, but they also know how to unblock or stimulate life energy if need be. They teach our philosophy and guide those who strive for self-knowledge. I think I would no longer be of this world if it hadn't been for their wisdom and their quiet strength. Without them, I wonder whether our peoples could have survived the terrible hardships of the last centuries.

I know that for certain readers, an existence such as ours might seem challenging and harsh. Yet, this is far from being the case. In fact, living symbiotically with nature *is* what humans fundamentally need. Human beings are a product of nature. With all their essence, they seek harmony with it. The nomadic life is a life of great liberty, in which the only laws that rule are those of the forest and a cordial understanding with those who coexist with it, including the fauna and flora.

❖

Anicinape families from our area are accustomed to resting on beds made of fresh fir branches (which give off an exquisite aroma!), and on big game pelts—either inside a tipi or a *capat8an*.[i]

At night, we're lulled to sleep by the sound of the fire which keeps us warm and safe. We sleep in direct contact with Mother Earth. This is truly a source of great energy. Getting weighed down by material goods and clutter is a real problem for nomads, since it makes moving around difficult. Because we have few belongings, the ones we do own—a blanket, a bowl, an ornament, or, of course, the various Sacred Medicine Items gifted to us over the years—become a little like cherished friends.

The door of a nomad's home is never locked. If a stranger happens by, we're not apprehensive, but rather cheerful at the prospect of meeting a new face. When one's nearest neighbours live kilometres away, one's notion of living space isn't quite the same as it is in a city. The daily rhythm of things isn't either. Consequently, there exists a natural predisposition to greet strangers and to make them feel welcome. Their arrival is not an intrusion, but a gift. In fact, a nomadic life is a life without stress. When white people first reached our lands, our concept of happiness, of well-being, and of health totally eluded the great majority of French colonists. Here is an excerpt from a letter written in 1691 by French interpreter Chrestien Le Clercq after conversing with a Chief belonging to the Mi'kmaq Nation.[ii] "Gentlemen" from New France, it seems, wanted to know why the "Savages" didn't wish to live or settle down in the European fashion:

> . . . some of our gentlemen of Isle Percée [. . .] were extremely surprised when the leading Indian, who had listened with great patience to everything I had said to him on behalf of these gentlemen, answered me in these words: [. . .] thou deceivest thyself greatly if thou thinkest to persuade us that thy country is better than ours. For if France, as thou sayest, is a

i A traditional hemicylindrical dwelling. Its arched frame is fashioned from young flexible trees. As with tipis, the *capat8an* was traditionally covered with big game skins or birch bark. With the arrival of Europeans, Anicinapek discovered cotton canvas and quickly adopted the material to envelop their homes with.

ii A First Nation belonging to the greater Algonquian family, established in the eastern regions of present-day Canada.

> little terrestrial paradise, art thou sensible to leave it? And why abandon wives, children, relatives, and friends? Why risk thy life and thy property every year, and why venture thyself with such risk, in any season whatsoever, to the storms and tempests of the sea in order to come to a strange and barbarous country which thou considerest the poorest and least fortunate of the world? [. . .] You are obliged to have recourse to the Indians, whom you despise so much, and to beg them to go a-hunting that you may be regaled. Now tell me this one little thing, if thou hast any sense: Which of these two is the wisest and happiest—he who labours without ceasing and only obtains, and that with great trouble, enough to live on, or he who rests in comfort and finds all that he needs in the pleasure of hunting and fishing? [. . .] Learn now, my brother, once for all, because I must open to thee my heart: there is no Indian who does not consider himself infinitely more happy and more powerful than the French. (Le Clercq 1910, 103-106)

This long-dead Mi'kmaq Chief's statement describes what our Elders would still attempt to explain if they were asked the same question today. In fact, on account of seeing white people breaking their backs chopping down trees in inexplicable quantities, from daybreak until nightfall without so much as a smile, Anicinapek ended up dubbing the French *8emitekoci*. This word, which is difficult to translate, evokes both the French's "wooden" faces (they never smiled), as well as their habit of felling trees for no apparent reason.

Three centuries later, Anicinapek and white people's concepts of prosperity and well-being are still contradictory. The only thing that has changed is the level of fatigue we share. Mother Earth is on the verge of irreversible depletion. What's more, a great many Anicinapek are worn down by their disconnect with nature. Generally speaking, it seems as though most humans simply cannot go on living with the levels of stress they are currently subjected to.

❖

Can you imagine a carefree existence? No need for you to balance any accounts or to plan ahead to live through tomorrow or the end of the month. A life in which you can live day to day. In which everyone has access to everything—food, clothes, shelter, heating, transportation . . . In which there are no rich or poor people. Each and every one of us deserves to eat and to feed our children, without worrying about the coming times. The forest bestows its bounty freely. The only thing we must offer in return is respect. Tell me, how could it be otherwise? When you hold a grouse in your hands, a being that has given up its life so that you may live, when you pluck its beautiful feathers, open its fragile body and find the twigs and bits of greenery still intact inside its stomach, what else is there to do than say to it: "*Mik8etc, mik8etc, mik8etc!*"?[i]

Every day, that very grouse fed on the purest of what Creator had to offer. It's the same for an Anicinape. How can one eat hare, beaver, or moose, or tan their hides, or sculpt their bones, and not feel infinitely grateful toward these magnificent creatures? When one's home is the entire forest, how can one not be attuned to the song of the wind in the trees, to the gliding of a canoe over calm waters, to the sight of a mother bear sauntering with her cubs, to the splendour of the sunrise or of the starry firmament? What in the entire world, I ask you, could ever make us any richer?

i "Thank you, thank you, thank you!" Pronounced "mig-wetch."

Second Fire

KAPITEOTAK: THE ONE WHOSE CRYING IS HEARD FROM AFAR

The second prophet said to the people:

> "You will know the Second Fire because at this time the nation will be camped by a large body of water. In this time the direction of the Sacred Shell will be lost. The Midewiwin will diminish in strength. A boy will be born to point the way back to the traditional ways. He will show the direction to the stepping stones to the future of the Anishinabe people."

–Edward Benton-Banai, *The Mishomis Book*

Anicinapek are not known for being a chatty sort. In fact, they never speak carelessly, or simply for the sake of carrying a conversation. As the great Dakota Chief Wabasha once advocated: "Guard your tongue in youth, and in age you may mature a thought that will be of service to your people!" (Eastman 2007, 23)

Our Elders' words blossom out of an inspired silence, and this grants these words great weight. My parents were no strangers to this rule. They supplied me with a great many useful teachings, and yet, they were frugal in regard to sharing their personal history. For this reason, I know practically nothing about how they met, besides the fact that it took place in the 1930s on the banks of the lovely Anakona Sipi—the "Biscuit River," dubbed so for the flat cookie-like pebbles found along its banks. White people understood the word as "Harricana" (which means nothing in our language), and named the river accordingly.

My mother, Emma Moé, belonged to the Cree Nation. She was born in 1913 at 8askakanic, where the Rupert River flows into the imposing James Bay. Emma was an extremely balanced woman and had a serious temperament. She was lavish with kisses and affection, and absolutely incapable of raising her voice to anyone at all.

My father, Tom Rankin, on the other hand, was of Mami8inni stock. Born at Lake Abitibi the same year as my mother, he came from a long line of Chiefs and Medicine Men that goes back to time immemorial. Before a political system modelled on that of white society was implemented in our communities, a traditional Chief had to study our ancestors' philosophy and Medicine. In our language, we call a Hereditary Chief "*Okima*," which white people translated into "Chief." Furthermore, they often qualified an *Okima*'s sons and daughters as "princes" and "princesses," but this interpretation is somewhat off the mark. These days, the political Chiefs of our Nations are styled *Okima*, but some of the term's historical subtleties have been lost. A true *Okima* is a sage, a counsellor, a pillar of his community. He knows how to speak the language of nature and his listening skills are unmatched. People do not speak to him to discuss finances, economic development, or political tactics. In fact, what my father passed down to me wasn't "power," but "Medicine." There's a considerable difference.

Furthermore, I feel it's important to mention that for us, Traditional Medicine is not only a man's prerogative. Women can also be destined for it. In truth, the way we see it, we are all born Medicine Men and Women. Some of us, however, are called upon to develop this knowledge and these practices. My father's experience and devotion to our ancestral wisdom made him a man whose Medicine proved to be very powerful.

At the time my parents were born, the fur trade was still alive and well. The Anakona River was the main transportation route between southern territories and James Bay, where British merchant ships came to replenish their holds with all kinds of pelts. Many Cree families were accustomed to travelling on this waterway regularly to transport merchandise from the south, where the Algonquins lived. It was through these interactions between the Cree and the Algonquins that my parents met and fell in love. They were married at Lake Abitibi and continued spending time at this place that had been so dear to my father's ancestors.

White people had already long been established at Matcite8eia, our summer meeting point on Lake Abitibi, where they operated trading posts. They knew that every year, they could find us there gathered in great numbers. Since we'd be returning from our trapping grounds, we always had nice pelts to trade. For a long time, the British who worked for the Hudson's Bay Company were the kings and masters of our lands. Thanks to the intelligence provided by First Nations, they were able to exploit the gigantic hydrographic network that reached the deepest corners of the Canadian forest. In the New France era, Frenchmen known as *coureurs de bois* or *voyageurs* undertook commercial transportation endeavours of their own, roving our vast country's meandering rivers at their great peril. When the British took over the territory, they resorted to the know-how of First Nations for these tasks. Unfortunately, Indigenous people were seldom fairly remunerated for transporting furs. After the merchandise reached its destination, the English would pay Anicinapek with litres and litres of liquor. Over the years, hundreds of those who had accepted this kind of work drowned on the return journey home.

Unlike our Innu brothers in the east, the majority of Algonquins kept their bartering with white people to a minimum. Upon discovering European products—items such as spices, cooking utensils, fabrics, footwear, and tools—we appreciated them. These goods and commodities were indeed practical, but we could do without them. In the eighteenth century, the fur trade moved toward our territories, to the Innu's detriment. Having depleted their animal resources and adopted European goods too quickly—to the point of becoming dependent on them—the Innu no longer knew how to look to the forest for sustenance and fell victim to many famines. Perhaps a similar outcome might have awaited us down the line, but it seems history had another set of challenges in mind for us.

Elders told me how they were wary of British trading practices. Since we didn't know how to read, His or Her Majesty's merchants would paint images of the items we coveted on a wall in their general stores: a bag of flour, a blanket, a rifle, and so on. The items were painted higher or lower on the wall according to their value. When an Anicinape entered the store, he was typically given a wooden rod whose length matched the height of his pelt pile. By placing this rod against the wall, he could see which products he could afford. Alas, the British had a compressing device that would shamelessly flatten the fruits of our labours. Hence, an Anicinape could never manage to deliver enough pelts to obtain the longer rod—the one that could reach the picture of the precious rifle.

We could also opt to trade our pelts for a paper voucher to be used for future purchases. According to the value of our furs, these vouchers were worth either "one pound" or "one shilling." However, the unsuspecting (and illiterate) Anicinape would be unaware that these tickets were only valid for a limited time. Many were conned, mistakenly under the impression that they would be able to purchase supplies and provisions in the months ahead. The Hudson's Bay Company's unscrupulous methods earned the British the nickname *Kimoti8inni* in the Algonquin language, which means "Thief People."

One day, the French set foot on the shores of Lake Abitibi. The British conquest of New France was a thing of the distant past. Canada, as an autonomous confederation, was now standing on its own two feet and the rules of the free market reigned. Thus, the Revillon Frères company was able to set up shop right across from the Matcite8eia British trading post. We quickly realized that doing business with the French was more pleasant than with the English. They paid us with real money, and, interestingly enough, were interested in managing the available resources properly. The fur trade had blown up into an immense industry by then, and had become completely unsustainable. Europeans prized beaver furs most of all, and used them for fashionable coats and hats. The result: Castoridae on our lands were facing extinction. By implementing trapping quotas and introducing a beaver species from Germany to our forests, we were able to save the genus, which thrives once again. These days still, there are two varieties of beavers in our country. Those with reddish coats are descendants of German beavers. When you come across a beaver with a darker brown pelt, on the other hand, you know without a doubt that you're dealing with a good old bona fide North American beaver.

❖

The summer meeting points for all the nomads in this country—whether Inuit or First Nations—were ideal gateways for men and women of God on evangelization missions. Little by little, from one conversion to the next, Christian traditions infiltrated our religious mores. Missionaries built churches next to trading posts, and wasted no time introducing mandatory baptisms and marriages. Elders belonging to my Nation could remember a time when, every summer, missionaries mustered all the single people and paired them off: "You, over there, come closer. You're going to marry this Indian here. And you, you'll do just fine for this man . . ." Men and women who had been perfect strangers the previous evening unexpectedly found themselves before an altar, vowing their undying faithfulness to one another.

Newborns received the sacrament of baptism in the same manner. Once a year, the priests gathered infants and summarily designated some white man or other as their godfather. Naturally, it was out of the question that an Indian could be considered for the role! This is how my great-great-grandfather came to be christened Collins Rankin, after a Scottish Hudson's Bay Company employee who probably happened to be passing through on baptism day. Since then, those of my lineage bear the name, even though there's not a drop of Scottish blood that flows through our veins. Due to the fact that there were lots of Scots and Englishmen in our region during this period, many of us bear last names such as Ruperthouse, McDougall, and McKenzie.

Likewise, around the same time, the French's fur trading efforts in Western Canada were meeting with great success, and today many First Nations families out there bear the names Larivière, Boudrias, or Delaronde despite the fact that they have no French blood at all.

❖

We are now in 1947—a dozen years have gone by since my parents married. Emma and T8amy (my father's given name in Anicinape) have given life to twelve beautiful children. Tragically, four of them have died, taken by sickness. In our territories, the encroachment of white traditions and politics is being felt more and more. Nonetheless, my parents enthusiastically go on living according to the nomadic ways bequeathed to them by their ancestors.

For the winter trapping and hunting season, they have settled with their children and a few other families in a place we call Kakicka8ak ("Where the waters are deep"), on the banks of Anakona Sipi. Emma is with child and her pregnancy is not going well—she's been losing blood for several weeks, which worries my father. Far from hospitals and so-called modern medicine, my mother is due to give birth in the heart of the forest once again. It'll be her thirteenth delivery, but not the last. She will, in time, give life to five more children!

That night, as usual, Emma and T8amy tell stories and sing lullabies to put the children to sleep. The fire purrs softly inside the small wood stove my father has set up near the entrance of our prospector tent. (For a few years now, many Anicinape families have adopted this new type of dwelling, which is just as easy to transport as a tipi but more spacious.) The wind has died down and a chorus of wolves is singing in the distance. Emma is about to let herself be lulled to sleep by the gentle chant, when all of a sudden, a contraction jolts her awake.

"T8amy! *8anickan!* Wake up!" she whispers into my father's ear, so as not to wake the children. "I've been worried since this morning—my belly tells me the baby's coming. The cramps weren't very bad, but they're getting worse. I really think that it's almost time."

"But the baby isn't yet due," my father says. "We're only expecting it in two moons."

"I know, but I think that we ought to warn the others. You should all prepare the tent for the delivery. I'll wake up *Kitci Jojo*, Grandmother Betsy."

When it comes to childbirth, both our women and our men are trained to help deliver babies and assist their mothers. And so, T8amy quickly gets dressed, pulls on his boots, and leaves to fetch Annie, the midwife, as well as her husband, Noye Kistabish, who is also well versed in our people's Medicine. If they pool their knowledge and experience, perhaps they'll be able to save the child and protect its mother in what bodes to be difficult circumstances.

A fire is lit in the tent reserved for ceremonies and medicinal purposes. Furs, blankets, hot water, and clean towels are brought inside. Annie prepares an alder bark-based decoction we give to women in labour—this Medicine helps mitigate hemorrhages. When Emma—held up by Grandmother Betsy—reaches the tent, her sacred water has already broken. The infant's arrival is imminent.

"Everything will be alright," my father tells her, trying his best to sound reassuring.

"I have faith in you all," says my mother, "but this time, I'll need *Kitci Manito*'s help as well as yours. It hurts more than usual. I'm worried for the baby."

"You're strong, Emma," replies Annie. "Don't let fear take over your body and spirit. We've seen babies survive at that age. I know you'll both be able to get through it."

A few hours later, Emma Moé and Tom Rankin's new son sees the light of day for the first time. This big, premature baby is none other than myself!

I may have given my mother grief—and then some—but to everyone's great relief, we're alive. I drink my fill, cradled snugly onto my mother's breast. However, I'm having difficulty breathing.

"It seems like his lungs aren't fully formed," note my father, Annie, and Noye.

"He'll live. I know he'll live," asserts my mother, before sinking into a deep slumber.

The wolves' chant has died down for a while now. The first rays of sunshine dance over the horizon. As with all his children, T8amy carries his well-bundled newborn to the outskirts of the camp and raises him in his arms to present him to the Great Spirit:

"I present you your new child, *Mino Manito*. Look after him. Give him your light so that he may become strong, and give him a good life."

Three weeks have gone by since my hectic birth. Things are still not looking good for me and my mother continues to lose a little blood. My father decides that we should head south before the streams stir from their beds of ice. And so, we all take our leave from Kakicka8ak and make for Lake 8akocik, where my mother's cousin Albert Moé—whom we called Okina8e—and *Kitci* Hendry normally set up camp with their families. Moreover, my father knows that white people sometimes land their metal birds on Lake 8akocik to trade with local communities. Perhaps they'll be able to help . . . In any case, a long trek awaits us—there are several dozen kilometres to cover before we reach our destination. Thankfully, we have our dogs to pull the sleds. Mom and I will ride in one alongside our belongings. The strongest members of our expedition will snowshoe there. Everyone's worried. Perhaps they've felt that a strange meeting with fate awaits us . . .

The journey has weakened us, my mother and I. With the help of the other adults in our group, my father was able to set up our new encampment. The beautiful days of *Sik8an* (pre-spring), with their generous rays of sunshine, will help us recover some of our strength. This morning, a few men left to search for food. Dad and Okina8e are chopping wood not far from our tent, when all of a sudden, a distinctive roar reverberates through the skies.

"*Ma?*" my father wonders out loud. "What's that noise?"

"It sounds like a metal bird," answers Okina8e. "It seems to be coming towards us. This might be your chance, T8amy."

Few of us from the Northern forests had seen these famed metal birds, which the *8emitekoci* often used for transportation. That day, however, this curious vehicle was indeed about to land by our home. This one was a floatplane fitted with skis for winter landings.

As we had hoped, the craft begins its descent on Lake 8akocik, but landing isn't easy. The frozen surface of the lake is streaked with snow drifts, which are making the manoeuvre difficult for the pilot in spite of his experience. All the same, guided by the smoke from our fires, the plane manages to alight and comes to a full stop in front of our encampment.

"*K8e k8e!*" the pilot calls out as he exits his bush plane—an old Canadian army aircraft. "*Ki mino matisin na?* You're doing all right?"

This man's name is George Polly. He knows our people well and gets by in our language. For several years now, George has been crisscrossing the skies over our forests with his trusty machine, trading his foodstuffs and commodities for our furs. Sometimes we use his airplane as a taxi when we need to reach the city quickly. The roar of his engines has attracted the attention of our entire little community, which gathers enthusiastically around him.

"*K8e k8e!*" answers my father, extending his hand. "*Pican*, come. Let's have some tea."

The pilot is invited to sit down near the twirling fire at the heart of the camp. After being handed a piping-hot cup of tea (there's always some tea boiling somewhere), George is asked about the latest news from the city. That day, however, my father isn't very talkative. Naturally, he is preoccupied by his beloved wife's health and that of his newborn son. After letting the adults chitchat with this rare visitor for a spell, my father decides that the opportune moment has come to ask what he's been meaning to ask. In his own language and—albeit clumsily—in the tongue of Shakespeare, he articulates what's been tormenting him for several weeks:

"*Akosi ni kokom, acitc ni kosis.* My wife's sick and so is my son. They aren't responding to our Medicine and I was praying for the Great Spirit's help. Perhaps He has sent you. Could you bring them with your plane to someplace where they could get white people's medicine?"

"I understand your situation, T8amy. I wish I could take them to the nearest hospital, but it would be a detour from my planned route. I won't have enough fuel to make it there."

The other men in my family jump in: "But we all have a little here, in these drums. We should be able to fill your tank."

The pilot had taken a few seconds to think it over, but being in the presence of my father—whom he held in high regard—he couldn't help but follow his heart. "It's risky. That'll give us a nasty mix of oil and fuel . . . But OK. Let's get going!"

Indeed, my father enjoyed an excellent reputation that reached even beyond our forests. All Anicinapek from our regions had heard of *Kitci* T8amy, the "Great Man." White people knew him as well, but by his Christian name, Tom Rankin. He had on many occasions dealt with them over clearing contracts, as Chief and spokesman of the Mami8inni Nation, or to negotiate some government agreement or other in the name of his people. Everywhere, among Anicinapek and white people alike, the great *Okima* Tom Rankin was highly valued for his listening skills, his calm, his sense of justice, and his endearing humour.

Without delay, my mother and I, as well as another woman in need of care, climb aboard the small airplane bound for the hospital in La Sarre. T8amy, with a twinge of pain in his heart, watches the craft as it begins to pick up momentum. But the big snow drifts on the lake complicate things. The metal bird starts bouncing on its makeshift runway, which stirs up the dangerous mixture of fuel oil and fuel. To the great distress of those who have stayed on solid ground, the worst happens: the aircraft catches fire. The more the pilot tries to lift the plane off the ground, the brighter the fire burns. Soon, all they can make out is a speeding fireball in the distance. Finally, it comes to a stop at the other end of the lake as the small horrified crowd cries out: "*Mi apan aca ki8itci anicinapeminanak!* That's it! It's the end for all those people!"

Spurred by his protective instinct, T8amy straps on his snowshoes and—without skipping a beat—races toward us. He's the first to reach the flaming airplane. Men must have been remarkably strong in those days—

or perhaps it was owing to a rush of adrenaline—because my father manages to rip the airplane door off its hinges with his bare hands. The men who've followed him have removed their snowshoes and are using them to shovel snow onto the burning fuselage.

My father has made it inside the craft, but the situation is dire. Everyone on board is unconscious. My mother's wearing her seatbelt, and I'm on her knees. He impulsively uproots our seat and that of the pilot. He also saves the poor sickly lady. Then, once everyone is outside, the plane finally drops through the broken ice and sinks into the murky waters below.

The men tend to my mother, the other woman, and the pilot, and help them regain the camp. As for me, I've stopped breathing. My body has turned blue. Knowing that my mother will be safe among the women, my father decides to stay with me in the woods. He lays me down on a bed of fir branches, lights a great Sacred Fire, and keeps a vigil over me until morning. I never did learn what transpired that night. He took his secret with him when he left for the Spirit World. In any event, a few hours after this dramatic incident, *Kitci* T8amy, the Great Man, had brought me back to life.

At sunrise, my eyes reopen, and this time my lungs are working at full steam. My wails resound through the forest as my father carries me in his arms back to camp. Meanwhile, my mother—who miraculously got through it all—is resting. Upon hearing my cries in the distance, she realizes that I'm once again alive. Between her sobs of joy and relief, she exclaims:

"*Aca Kapiteotak citcic takocin!* Here comes the child whose crying is heard from afar!"

Since that improbable day, Elders have called me Kapiteotak, "The one whose crying is heard from afar." It can also mean "The one whose singing (or grumbling) is heard from afar." One or the other! Incidentally, the name was also once bestowed upon my paternal great-grandfather, because, by all accounts, his loud singing accompanied him wherever he went.

Afterward, as was customary, I was baptized and christened Dominique by Catholic missionaries. That said, all those who know me intimately know what an important thread the name Kapiteotak is to the tapestry of my life as a Medicine Man.

This mysterious thread didn't escape the keen gaze of our Elders. They immediately recognized meaningful signs in the circumstances of my first days on Earth. They said: "This child's destiny will be different from other children, for at birth, he received two lives. One was given to him by his mother, and the other, by his father." In their eyes, these events seemed to point to the fact that I should succeed my father as Hereditary Chief. The years that followed would soon provide them with proof of that.

Third Fire

MY FIRST EAGLE FEATHER

The third prophet said to the people:

> "In the Third Fire, the Anishinabe will find the path to their chosen ground, a land in the West to which they must move their families. This will be the land where food grows on water."
>
> –Edward Benton-Banai, *The Mishomis Book*

My seventh summer will forever be etched in my memory. I suppose that my impressions of this period are more vivid because I'd reached the age when I was becoming a little man. But it's also because this was to be the last tranquil summer I would spend with my family—we just didn't know it at the time. We were now living between the town of Amos and Lake Abitibi, since the authorities no longer allowed us to call the woods home. Dad had found work in the small municipality of Saint-Marc-de-Figuery, about twenty kilometres south of Amos. He and several other Anicinapek were involved in the construction of a new building—a school, by the looks of it. The *8emitekoci* were proud of these big square boxes, in which they taught all sorts of things that didn't seem very useful in our eyes. At any rate, Anicinape workers earned modest wages at these jobs, which helped them feed their families. What these men didn't know, however, is that the very walls they were putting up would soon become their own children's prison.

❖

For the time being, though, we still managed to spend some lovely summer days in the forest, where we'd meet up with other Anicinape families. Whether we were on our winter or summer grounds, I loved following Elders deep into the woods when they sought out food or Medicine. No one made a big deal of my fate to one day lead as Hereditary Chief, but all the same, I felt that I was considered different from other children. I could tell that I was being protected from outside influences, which we were feeling more and more.

I often slept over at the homes of other Grandfathers and Grandmothers. In our communities, children have quite a bit of liberty. Indeed, it was normal for me to leave for a few days on excursions with different *Kitci*—those we call Grandmother, Grandfather, or Elders for their wisdom: *Kitci* Andrew, *Kitci* Tcotep, *Kitci* William Black . . . One would take me to the traplines; another would invite me to pick berries, while teaching me about the behaviours of different wild animals; and yet another would teach me how to find my bearings in the woods:

"Look around you. Observe the trees and tell me if you can see some in the distance that appear different from the others."

"I can see a patch of sparser and smaller trees over there."

"Precisely. Those trees are precious points of reference. If you follow their direction, you'll come across a lake or a river. There, you'll find life. That's the safest place for human beings. You don't need to fret if it takes you a while to find your way. The forest can provide you with everything you need for days and days. Keep fear, worry, and solitude out of your mind. Instead, enjoy yourself. Think of the animals, like *Mak8a*, the Bear, or *Mahikan*, the Wolf. Do you think they feel lost in the forest? Like them, learn to feel at ease where you are, surrounded by the trees, the birds, and the other creatures who call this place home—just the same as you."

Of course, accompanying grown-ups when they hunted and trapped required me to be acquainted with death. These Grandfathers and Grandmothers taught me to respect animals as much as humans, to pray and to thank them when they had agreed to give up their lives to us. They made me see that in reality, death doesn't exist—forms merely change. "When an animal gives up its life," they would tell me, "understand that in fact, life goes on. The animal exists within you, for it nourishes you. Its fur, its skin, and its bones go on living in a different form, thanks to the clothes, tools, or toys they become."

❖

Most of the time, however, if I left on an adventure, it would be with my father. He enjoyed taking me to the far end of Lake Abitibi. The *8emitekoci* had traced a border right down the middle of this great, sacred body of water, consequently separating what they called the provinces of Quebec and Ontario. To us, the earth—*aki*—isn't divisible. Borders couldn't separate humans any more than they could separate fauna or flora. Our Anicinape brothers who were camped here and there around the lake spoke the same language as we did and belonged to the same people—even though their dialects were slightly different. Some called them the Otcip8e.

And so, Dad and I would leave on canoe trips for a few days at a time. After every leg, we'd find a perfect place to spend the night somewhere ashore. Then, we'd light a fire and prepare our overnight camp.

"Give yourself everything," Dad would remind me, as he'd set up camp. "If you know how to observe and respect nature, it'll bestow its gifts on you and give you a good life. If the weather's bad, stay inside your shelter where you'll be dry and warm. When the weather's mild, gather everything you need for your well-being. You don't ever have to suffer from the cold, hunger, thirst, or anything else. Give yourself everything, Kapiteotak."

When the sun went down, we'd paddle over the calm waters of the lake and visit the beaver dams and lodges. I'd sit in the front and my father would steer the craft from the back.

"Anicinapek are nomadic because of the Beaver," Dad would explain as he rowed. "Every autumn, at the first snow, it's important to visit their lodges to see how many of them remain. If there are only a few young ones left, it means that the time has come for us to move our camp to someplace where we'll find a lot of adult beavers."

"Otherwise we'll wipe them out," I ventured.

"That's right. An Anicinape must look after his territory and the spirits that inhabit it. The beaver is one of the most important animals to our survival. Its meat is extremely nourishing. Its pelt and bones are very useful. We also dry out its sacs for four or five months—the time it takes for the Medicine they contain to ferment and acquire its full potency. Once they turn black, they're ready to lend us their powerful Medicine. White people have what they call penicillin to disinfect wounds or to numb injuries. We have beaver glands."

I can still picture us, Dad and I, on the shores of the lake, far from our family camp. The sun has just gone down and we've finished our meal of grilled *kinoce.*[i] Dad finishes washing our stoneware dishes and mugs, and tells me to get in the water:

"*A8sa, pican!* Come on, get over here! Take off your clothes. *Pakopin*, get in the water—I want to show you something."

Without so much as a peep, I oblige him, all too happy to take a dip in the lake's inviting waters on this gentle late August evening.

"At this time of year, beavers are rather fat," my father tells me from the beach. "They've eaten so well these past weeks that they're covered with an oil that ends up in the water. We can't see it from shore, because it doesn't float. But notice, you can feel it under the surface of the water."

"*Tep8e na?* Really? . . . Ah, yes! I can feel it now!"

"This oil had medicinal properties. It can greatly benefit people who have skin problems."

Suddenly, not far too away from us, we hear the distinctive sound of a beaver tail slapping the water's surface.

"Here we go. They're getting to work now," announces my father. "Swim slowly toward the middle of the lake. Don't make a wake and stay calm. They'll get curious about you and will want to find out who you are."

Dad's right. Within a few minutes, I'm surrounded by a dozen beavers who gingerly come and go as they please to get a better look at me. The adults are all much too busy either carrying tasty branches to feed their young, or regaining the shore to take down a big tree. But the younger ones

i Pike.

are full of curiosity. We splash around a bit to get to know one another. It's absolutely delightful.

Meanwhile, my father has taken a seat by the campfire. "*Kapiteotak, ki wi nipa na?* Kapiteotak, do you want to sleep?" he asks.

"*Ehe! Nokom ni ka pica.* Yes, I'll be right there."

Dad's waiting for me on our bed of fir branches, under the lean-to we're using as a temporary shelter. Behind the fire, he's built a short reflector wall that redirects the heat toward us. It's nice and toasty in our little den. All night, Dad will tend to the fire for me. It's a man's responsibility. When I grow up, I too will tend to the fire for my wife and children. But for the moment, I'm still a little boy. My body and soul are warm and comfortable, and I'm in the arms of my father who's speaking in a soft voice. It's gently guiding me to the world of dreams.

"*Amik*, the Beaver, is a great teacher," he whispers. "If you destroy his dam or his house, he'll rebuild it that very same night. You'll never wear down his patience. He'll never allow humans to destroy the Medicine destined to feed and protect his young. Whatever challenges you encounter in life, do as he does—never give up. Always remember the teaching of the Beaver, my son. Don't ever forget it."

In my tender youth, that is to say the 1950s, Quebec Premier Maurice Duplessis governed the province with an iron fist. Many historians have dubbed this era the "*Grande Noirceur*"—the Great Darkness—for the sentiment of fear that reigned among both Québécois people and First Nations who coexisted on the same territory. This hot-tempered politician often suppressed civil rights. Under his rule, the Church was given full powers over anything related to schools, universities, and hospitals. What's more, the clergy and the authorities worked together toward a common goal.

Everyone—white and Indigenous people alike—feared being reprimanded by the parish priest if they didn't walk the straight and narrow, righteous path. Those living in big cities enjoyed a bit more freedom, but in small communities, the influence of religious figures could be a frightful thing—especially if one came across an authoritative individual, or a downright twisted one. Back home, this pressure was felt twice as hard: white people were not only trying to reshape our religious beliefs, but also attempting to convert us to their way of life.

In the beginning, their efforts to change our customs were relatively innocuous. I remember, for instance, how we were encouraged to eat corned beef. The missionaries had hoped that by introducing us to these canned goods, we wouldn't need to go off into the woods to find food as frequently. And yet, that beef was so foul-tasting! We sincerely wondered how it could be that the *8emitekoci* preferred this strange, metal-packaged substance to healthy, naturally-smoked fish and meats. Meanwhile, the Hudson's Bay Company traders convinced us to buy their second-hand motor-fitted boats. "This way," they'd proudly say, "you can hunt all day and be back home by evening!" What they didn't realize was that the noise from the motor scares game away, that fuel leaks inevitably contaminate our rivers, and that portages become a lot more tiring when we have a motor to carry—not to mention all those corned beef tins in our backpacks! Certainly, Anicinapek enjoyed racing up and down rivers at full throttle, but not all of them grasped to what degree this accelerating rhythm of life would soon not only poison Mother Earth, but also the human spirit.

In short, most of the time, white people imposed their ways on us in good faith, and we gradually incorporated these things into our lives. In their eyes, every single conversion to Christianity and modernity represented one step closer to a completely justified assimilation. Besides, the authorities had no tolerance for the nomadic lifestyle of these "Savages" who lived as they saw fit deep in the woods. Alas, they didn't like to see us among the general public either. Meanwhile, the federal government's *Indian Act* was in full swing, in addition to an assortment of local rules. These, for instance, barred us from entering this or that restaurant, prevented us from taking a bus or a taxi, or made it impossible for us to rent a room at a particular hotel. We had to find a way to exist amid these contradictions: respecting laws and rules and submitting to the power of the Church—which was closely linked to police powers—all while trying to survive by the means we knew and loved!

That said, many priests had learned Indigenous languages and appreciated our way of life. They led by example and had passed on their Christian values to our parents. As was common at the time, our people would go to church during summer gatherings, where the priests awaited them every year. By dint of being constantly exposed to imagery of Hell and the Devil, Anicinapek had ended up fearing these negative influences and sought to protect themselves from them. Our very pious mothers, for the most part, had learned to love the Father, the Son, and the Holy Ghost, and to pray the white way. Many men, on the other hand, would simply wait until they were deep in the woods to hold their traditional ceremonies away from the white eye. Even though she enjoyed praying the Rosary and attending Mass, my mother still fully respected our own ancestral beliefs, and practised them. As for my father, he didn't find it difficult to follow the Church's Commandments while simultaneously upholding our traditions. The stakes were high, however. Medicine Men and Women were seen as sorcerers and witches, and whoever was caught practising our beliefs risked getting arrested. This actually happened to my father. Whenever someone reported him for having taken part in a traditional ceremony or ancestral rites, the authorities would threaten him with jail, without so much as a trial.[i] I remember even joining him behind bars on one occasion when I was young, because we had been caught with our Sacred Bundles somewhere in the Low Bush region.

i In 1884, the Canadian government amended the *Indian Act* in order to ban Potlatchs. These large ceremonial feasts helped provide a sense of unity among First Nations and were occasions during which they would practise many important traditions. Under this new law, dances and ceremonies were prohibited, while Sacred Bundles and Objects were confiscated or destroyed.

It was against this background of enforced conformity and omnipresent fear that I received my first Eagle Feather. It may have been many years ago, but I can still remember the details of that momentous day. "*Pican!* Come!" my father had said. "We're going to visit the Low Bush Elders!" When it came to accompanying my father on an adventure, I never had to be asked twice. Low Bush was on the Ontario side of Lake Abitibi. My father enjoyed dropping in on his Otcip8e friends there whenever he had the chance. This time, we left in a motorboat along with some Elders from our community, including *Kitci-Papa* (my grandfather Jim), *Kitci* Hendry, *Tcomitc* Black, and the members of the Nadeau family. We crossed the lake and upon reaching Low Bush, were given a most warm welcome by the Elders there. We chatted about this and that, and then they invited us to take a seat around the Sacred Fire. It was late in the afternoon on a midsummer day. The air was fresh. The women prepared the evening meal nearby. I can remember that around our Circle, poles had been planted at the four directions of the compass. Feathers and skulls from guardian Spirits of the forest hung from the trees. And then, an eagle feather was passed from hand to hand.

"The Eagle Feather," began an Elder, "is a reward for the one who receives it. The Eagle teaches us the power of the Circle. He climbs very high in the sky, always circling. He is free, but he must constantly keep his balance by relying on the wind. His gaze is piercing. He can see clearly despite his distance. As he climbs higher in the sky, he acts as a messenger between us and Creator."

At this point, to my great surprise, the Elder asked me to approach him.

"Kapiteotak, this Eagle Feather is for you. You'll have to keep it safe always. It'll accompany you in your all ceremonies. Whenever you speak in the Circle of Elders, you'll have to hold it up straight, as a token of respect for the Eagle and those who are listening to you. It'll inspire you to speak with strength, clarity, and balance. You'll also have to keep it hidden. For the time being, this Feather will be our secret—just between you and us. One day, you'll be able to display it in public without fear."

Even though I was only seven, I understood well that this was an important sign of acknowledgment and a welcome gesture on behalf of the Elders. It's sad to say, but what I remember most is that I was beset with fear. "Why me?" I thought. "Why expose me to all these dangers?" I liked the feeling of being surrounded and protected by Elders, and I loved receiving their teachings, but sometimes I wished that I could be like other children—carefree and unburdened by these many responsibilities.

For a long time—*a very long time*—I was torn by my obligation to practise our beliefs in the utmost secrecy. We travelled, moved, and lived under the scrutiny of priests, the authorities, and Anicinapek who had completely converted to Catholicism. I even had to hide my Feather from many individuals who were close to me. But in the end, I kept it safe. My mother always hid it under her bed or in one of her many small wooden chests. When I grew up and left the nest, I took it with me, but I didn't dare show it in public until an assembly in 1985, when I was thirty-eight years old.

I was still a young boy and an outsider when I received my first Eagle Feather, and it would take me quite some time before I understood that my condition was not a curse.

Fourth Fire

THE BIBLE AND THE LAND

The Fourth Fire was originally given to the people by two prophets. They came as one. They told of the coming of the Light-skinned Race.

One of the prophets said:

> "You will know the future of our people by what face the Light-skinned Race wears. If they come wearing the face of nee-kon'-nis-i-win' (brotherhood), then there will come a time of wonderful change for generations to come. They will bring new knowledge and articles that can be joined with the knowledge of this country. In this way two nations will join to make a mighty nation. This new nation will be joined by two more so that the four will form the mightiest nation of all. You will know the face of brotherhood if the Light-skinned Race comes carrying no weapons, if they come bearing only their knowledge and a handshake."

The other prophet said:

> "Beware if the Light-skinned Race comes wearing the face of ni-boo-win' (death). You must be careful because the face of brotherhood and the face of death look very much alike. If they come carrying a weapon . . . beware. If they come in suffering . . . they could fool you. Their hearts may be filled with greed for the riches of this land. If they are indeed your brothers, let them prove it. Do not accept them in total trust. You shall know that the face they wear is the one of death if the rivers run

with poison and fish become unfit to eat. You shall know them by these many things."

–Edward Benton-Banai, *The Mishomis Book*

There is a well-known saying on the African continent that aptly encapsulates its colonial experience: "When the missionaries came to Africa, they had the Bible and we had the land. They said 'let us close our eyes and pray.' When we opened them, we had the Bible, and they had the land."

It's uncanny how this quote, popularized by both Archbishop Desmond Tutu, recipient of the Nobel Prize, and politician Jomo Kenyatta, the late father of modern Kenya, resembles our own . . .[i] When I was a child, the evangelical work brought to our lands by Catholic missionaries had already been ongoing for several hundred years. Slowly but surely, many Anicinapek felt as though it might be better to adopt the white people's God and to pray to Jesus. After enduring all these woes, perhaps this white-bearded Creator would be able to eliminate our suffering, our ancestors told themselves.

Nearly five centuries ago, white men reached our shores after spending many long months at sea. When they disembarked from their huge wooden ships, they were in a sorry state. To travel in this way—without fresh food or water, without being able to bathe, exclusively in the company of other men, and for such a long duration—was inconceivable to us. It's no surprise that all manner of critters and disease—rats, lice, sexually transmitted infections, scurvy, and the like—had gotten off the ships along with them!

Their spirits were also tainted. These men lived under the shadow of fear and greed, and they seemed to need to get drunk off their "firewater" constantly, in the hopes of turning their thoughts to anything else. When they sobered up, they regretted their mistakes and fixated on their inner demons. At that point, they strove to numb themselves not with alcohol, but with ready-made prayers that they would recite incessantly until their malaise temporarily subsided.

---

i Although this quote is often attributed to either of these great African leaders, it seems to originate from Rolf Hochhuth's controversial play, *The Deputy, a Christian Tragedy* (1964).

At first, we welcomed these strange men and cared for them. We fished and hunted for them. We dressed them, and offered them firewood so they could keep warm. We showed them our remedies and shared the Sacred Pipe with them. Some appreciated our lifestyle and understood our vision, but others, stubborn and hungry for power, were stuck in their ways. So much so, in fact, that the corruption that tormented their bodies and spirits eventually spread to our own people. Beforehand, our Elders had lived long and healthy lives. The arrival of Europeans on our continent—it must be said—heralded the advent of disease, destruction, and death. "*Iak8a ockiakosi8in!* Beware of new diseases!" our Elders would warn, when discussing the evil spirits hiding in the white man's luggage. The wisest and most perceptive among us could see what was coming. They understood that we had to limit our contact with these strange characters who thought of nothing but their expansionist plans. These Elders knew that they'd have to protect their children's souls against the coming waves of harmful influences.

For several generations, my ancestors were able to carry on living their nomadic lifestyle in relative peace, far from the frantic world of white people. Only the ravages of alcohol managed to infiltrate the confines of the forest, for although white men were not yet truly interested in our faraway lands, their inventions still found their way upriver, and soon began inexorably affecting the most fragile of our families. The magnificent equilibrium our ancestors had taught us to respect and to admire was thus shattered.

The *coup de grâce* befell us the day the governments decided to stop tolerating the ancient nomadic lifestyle practised by a segment of the Canadian population. The time had come to civilize Indians and Inuit, and to force them to settle down by any means necessary, starting with the 1876 *Indian Act*. This act of Parliament would thereafter introduce a series of increasingly restrictive measures that ultimately aimed to assimilate our peoples.

As far as Inuit are concerned, the authorities who were in charge between the 1950s and 1970s found an ingenious and cruel method to persuade the Northern nomads to settle down in the villages created for them—by sending out Royal Canadian Mounted Police officers to shoot their faithful sled dogs in cold blood. For decades—up until recently—the RCMP denied committing this massacre despite consistent testimonies from my Northern brothers and sisters that maintained the contrary. In any case, as a result, many suddenly found themselves unable to fish or hunt on the tundra, and the Northern nomadic lifestyle came to an abrupt end. From coast to coast, an entire generation of Inuit can still recall the terrible moment the men returned home in tears to announce the dire news to their wives: "The police killed our dogs. What'll become of us?" Or the women crying out in every community: "How will we feed our children? Our husbands don't speak the white people's language. They don't know any trades besides hunting. They haven't learned to wield the white man's tools, which are needed to maintain the houses that the government forces us to live in. They only know how to build iglus and set up summer tents. Oh, how happy we were, living freely in the great outdoors!"

As Chief, my father took part in many meetings and negotiations with the governments of his era. The leaders of his generation were forced to deal with the most restrictive treaties of all. "We always welcomed the white man's representatives into our tents," he'd often say, "but invariably, by the time they got out, we had lost more lands."

These negotiations, in which our peoples no longer had any power, ended up tearing us away from the forest. As far as our community—that of the Mami8inni—is concerned, the government had promised us houses if we agreed to give up our nomadic lifestyle right then and there. We agreed. We renounced our rich and rewarding existence in the heart of nature. Alas, the housing we were promised would only be built ten years later! During those long years of waiting and powerlessness, we were forced to establish ourselves in camps on the outskirts of Amos. However, even this bothered the *8emitekoci* townsfolk, and we were thereafter repeatedly relocated. The first time, our families had to move to the banks of the Harricana River, which was then being used for log driving. The logging companies were cutting down trees in enormous quantities, making it almost impossible to navigate those waters by canoe. On top of that, the water was extremely polluted. Eventually, we were displaced to make way for a new sawmill, and so we established ourselves on the opposite bank.

A while later, they pushed us back to an area we called Kaicpakoiak —"The Tall Firs." The water there had been so polluted by the logging industry that it contaminated the fish we depended on to survive, and led to severe cases of mercury poisoning. Several dozens of our people died as a result.

In those years, at Kaicpakoiak, my father was hired by the government to help build the new Route 117, which would run between Mont-Laurier and Senneterre. After the project was completed, my father received a visit from Hervé Larivière, the Indian agent. Brandishing a letter from the government, the man instructed us to vacate the premises, because the presence of Indians would bother tourists who wished to visit the Abitibi.

At that point, religious authorities agreed to accommodate us on the lands of the Amos diocese. I can still remember this "temporary" encampment and the nuns there. They would occasionally lower us buckets of food from their high balconies with a rope and a pulley, for we had difficulty supporting ourselves at the time.

Shortly thereafter, we were evicted once again to allow for the construction of a convent for cloistered nuns. Some families went back to the other side of the river, while others managed to rent less-than-pristine houses in town. My father was one of the first among the latter to pull this off, for few white people were willing to take us in as tenants. After all, I suppose, the concepts of "rent" and "bills" were completely foreign to us. In fact, they were inconceivable—according to our philosophy, the right to shelter, food, and clothes applies to everyone, without exception. Everyone should have the right to "give themselves everything" freely, in accordance with the riches of Mother Earth and what she can provide. How could humans "own" the Earth? Isn't it us, rather, who belong to Her?

Our vagrancies only came to an end in 1961. Worn out from constantly having to negotiate for some new spot or other to camp out on, my father agreed to sign a deal with the federal and provincial governments of Diefenbaker and Duplessis, in order to settle the question of our definitive settlement once and for all. Having come to the same conclusion as my father, thousands of Indigenous leaders across the country followed suit. This is how First Nations reserves came to be. Ours, which was named Pikogan,[i] was established on a two-square-kilometre tract of land north of Amos. It was actually an old farmstead, which the government had bought and given to our families. My father was the first to settle in. The government subsequently erected other houses on the property, which families gradually moved into. When the reserves were first created, First Nations were required to move into them, but shortly thereafter, the ban that prohibited us from living elsewhere was lifted. As for me, I lived in Pikogan during my late teenage years, but I got out of there as soon as I could. I felt that if I were ever to find freedom, it would be outside the reserve—even if I would need to work twice as hard to earn it.

Before 1961, in the years leading up to the establishment of our reserve, the situation had become tedious and complex for those of us who were still waiting for permission to finally live *somewhere*. We weren't allowed to live in the forest like we had in the past, and we were unwelcome anywhere else. In town, we struggled daily with contradictory rules. We were expected to become sedentary, and yet, we weren't allowed to patronize public places such as grocery stores, markets, hotels, or restaurants. Furthermore, we were barred from using public transport—buses, taxis, and trains. Whenever the *8emitekoci* needed our labour, they assigned us to segregated train wagons and made special stops along the railway, to drop us off far away from the white public eye.

I must have been six or seven when our family first moved to Amos. Moving to town meant that we had to adapt to white people's square structures. This was a difficult thing for us, who favoured the power of the circle in all its incarnations. The first time I entered a house, I felt claustrophobic. I couldn't stop eyeing the ceiling, fearing that it would collapse. "How does it stay up there above our heads—all on its own?"

i Pikogan means "Tipi village." Early on, the reserve was simply called Abitibi8inni.

I asked myself. "And how does one keep warm here in the winter? I don't see a firepit in this *miki8am!*"[i] Elders had always taught us that the spirit is at ease in a tipi. Thanks to a tipi's round base, energy can circulate freely, with no obstacles. (After all, don't "circle" and "circulate" share an etymological root in your language?) In these *8emitekoci miki8aman*, with their rigid walls and sharp corners, we had the impression that the spirit would constantly be bumping into things!

At first, we were so ill at ease in our square box that my father set up a tent in the backyard. Most of my brothers and sisters, like me, refused to sleep in the house. We needed to be in direct contact with Mother Earth and to breathe in the fresh night air. We weren't the only ones. Nearly all Anicinapek who had moved to town did the same. When the cold season approached, however, Dad had to convince us to sleep inside, as the tent wasn't heated.

❖

My first encounters with the *8emitekoci* turned out to be somewhat challenging. The language barrier wasn't a problem the first time I mingled with a group of white kids, because all of Earth's children tend to play the same spontaneous, unscripted games. But racism was widespread in those days. It didn't take long for some older boys to come up with the brilliant idea to lead me down the town streets and leave me there. They fled in laughter, just so they could play a mean old trick on this poor little Indian boy fresh from the woods. A son of the forest like me will always know how to find his bearings in nature, but in the meandering streets of an unfamiliar town, I was completely disoriented. (If truth be told, I still struggle in big cities, even in those I visit often. It comes with the proverbial job, I suppose!)

I wandered for hours hoping to find my way home, but I had no point of reference. Instinctively, I closed in on the river which flowed through the heart of town, without realizing that I was actually moving farther away from our home.

---

i House.

Night fell and it started to rain. I took shelter under the veranda of a white house and stayed there a while, shivering. Thankfully, someone ended up noticing me through the gaps between the stairs. Before long, several nice ladies had come outside and were speaking to me in their language. I was afraid and stayed there, tucked in my corner. One of them had the idea of offering me a glass of milk and some cookies. I was terribly hungry, so I followed them inside their *miki8am*. That was the first time I tasted cow's milk and chocolate cookies, and frankly, it was delicious!

In fact, blind chance had led me to the porch of a house belonging to religious Sisters. They entrusted me to the police, who tracked down my father in no time, as he was one of the few Anicinapek to live within the town limits in those days. Our reunion was an emotional one. When I returned home, I was assailed with a barrage of kisses and everyone wanted to hear about my latest caper. My mother and sisters hugged me incessantly and offered me all kinds of delicious treats. That night, cozily tucked under a nice big pile of blankets, I even slept in a real bed—which was quite a privilege back then, because there weren't enough in the house to go around!

In this fashion, we started to learn about "modern" living. We had to pick up on the habits and customs of people who rejected us, and because our survival depended on it, imitate them as best we could. Some *8emitekoci* changed sidewalks to avoid crossing paths with us. Others, however, proved compassionate and affable.

One day, Father Deschênes, a priest who spoke our language and who was fond of my parents, offered to show us Amos's great cathedral. Curious, we accepted his invitation and hopped into his truck—there was me, my parents, and two of my sisters. Once we stepped inside the imposing church, we were stunned. We had never seen anything like it. All those carved stone blocks piled on top of one another! All that gold, those sculptures, those paintings! I was speechless under the huge dome that crowned this gigantic house of prayer. After all, I was already baffled as to how the ceiling of our hovel could possibly stay in place! Our friend Father Deschênes made us take a seat near the door in the last row of pews, and joined the clergy at the front of the church. Out of the blue, a woman drew near and insulted us. We couldn't understand her words, but she was clearly infuriated. She spouted invectives at my mother and grabbed her by the coat to pull her away from the pew. Unable to articulate in French that it was the priest who had seated us there, my mother tried to break away from the woman's claws. Then, the woman spat on my mother.

Note that at the time, Catholics in Quebec could "buy" their pews. It was another of the clergy's ideas, as the Church was constantly looking for new ways to cover its outrageous spending habits. Later, we were told that Father Deschênes had sat us down in the lady's pew. All the same, this *8emitekoci* had spat on my mother, who was such a gentle and respectful woman. After witnessing this scene, I was beside myself. Even though I was very young, I already possessed a warrior's temper. Seething with anger at this extreme insult, and pained by the fact that we would never be understood by these humans who despised us, I stormed out of the white people's cathedral in a huff.

My parents were more magnanimous, and they attended church for the rest of their lives. I must admit that for me, this episode was a revelatory one, and it hinted at the all-too-numerous inconsistencies one finds in the Church. I've remained mindful of this. I still occasionally pray in church and I like the message of Christ, but I have a hard time coming to terms with what some people have done with it. I encourage everyone to cherish the faith they grew up with, but I also believe that one must remain clearheaded regarding the spiritual when it falls into the traps of closed-mindedness, inequality, dogma, rules and regulations, expansionism, faulting and punishments, fear, or losing touch with reality. When the head topples the heart and common sense, all dangers risk coming true. What follows starkly illustrates this.

❖

The silence that surrounds suffering is more painful than the suffering itself. We have now reached the point where this silence must be broken as we broach the darkest subject of this story: the residential schools for Indian children.

To the residential school survivors out there, who have known all conceivable violations, understand that our only option is to heal ourselves, but that in order to heal, we must traverse the wall of the unspoken. To the authors of the crimes committed in the schools who are perhaps reading this book—you never know!—healing through frank speech is also your only solution. To all the silent witnesses to these crimes, that is to say all Canadians, understand that a festering wound must be reopened and cleansed before it can heal. We must all have the courage to unearth this sad episode of our past if we hope to truly reconcile, if we want to move on to a new chapter in our shared existence.

One who fears facing one's own emotions is a caged being. No matter our wounds, the worst thing anyone can do is to try to forget without screaming or weeping. Countless cries and tears have escaped my body to pave the way for my healing. I still bear the scar, and it can awaken every now and then, but I've managed to accept the unacceptable and to forgive the unforgivable. Writing these memoirs requires me to relive once again the details of this period of my youth, but I believe that this exercise simply constitutes another step in the process toward liberating myself from the past. And so, I'm doing this for myself, but I'm also doing this because I'm convinced that it's something we must collectively go through. By "collectively," I mean all those who, from a distance or intimately, experienced the residential school episode, because it's high time for the inhabitants of this country—Indigenous and non-Indigenous alike—to learn to know and understand each other.

Finally, I also hope that anyone who has ever known any kind of suffering in the face of life's challenges can be inspired by our story, because sooner or later, we all have to prevail over old wounds from our pasts.

Fifth Fire

THE GREAT TEAR

The fifth prophet said:

> "In the time of the Fifth Fire there will come a time of great struggle that will grip the lives of all Native people. At the waning of this Fire there will come among the people one who holds a promise of great joy and salvation. If the people accept this promise of a new way and abandon the old teachings, then the struggle of the Fifth Fire will be with the people for many generations. The promise that comes will prove to be a false promise. All those who accept this promise will cause the near destruction of the people."

When the Fifth Fire came to pass, a great struggle did indeed grip the lives of all Native people. The Light-skinned Race launched a military attack on Indian people throughout the country aimed at taking away their land and their independence as a free and sovereign people. It is now felt that the false promise that came at the end of the Fifth Fire was the materials and riches embodied in the way of life of the Light-skinned Race. Those who abandoned the ancient ways and accepted this new promise were a big factor in causing the near-destruction of the Native people of this land.

–Edward Benton-Banai, *The Mishomis Book*

It was a late-summer morning like many others. Mom was probably busy preparing her *panik*. Dad might have been making a pair of snowshoes or a *tikinakan* for the baby on the way. I don't know exactly—I was only eight years old at the time and my memories of that painful day are pretty vague. However, I clearly remember seeing an RCMP officer and a representative from the Department of Indian Affairs appear out of nowhere. That day, contrary to their routine, they weren't there for the grown-ups, but rather for the children.

"Mr. and Mrs. Rankin, we've been ordered to take six of your children to the new Saint-Marc-de-Figuery Indian Residential School. If you resist, you'll be breaking the law."

Our poor parents were caught off-guard. My father must have thought: "It's that building they made us work on last year. So . . . that school was intended for our own children!" Our cries and our attempts to escape were all for naught. That morning, my powerless parents were robbed of the most precious thing they had left: their children.

So here we are, crammed into a bus, headed for an unknown destination. There's my brother Willy, four of my sisters, many other Anicinape children, and myself. Terrified, we weep. After several minutes, we come to a halt in front of a large building surrounded by fields as far as the eye can see—the residential school for Indian children. We're unceremoniously separated from our sisters, who, led by the Sœurs de Saint-François d'Assise, disappear into the girls' wing. We boys are to be entrusted to the Oblates.

We can't understand what's happening to us. These men and women garbed in black speak to us in an incomprehensible language. We cross a large room where other Anicinape children are seated in rows. Their hair has been cut off and they're all wearing the same uniform.

I'm suddenly given a burlap sack. Men remove my clothes and sit me down naked in a barber chair. In one fell swoop, they shave my head. I break into tears as my father's teachings echo in my mind and in my heart:

"Your hair speaks to your life energy. They're the antennae that keep you in communion with the Earth. In our tradition, men let their hair grow out to show the bond they share with Mother Earth, and also with women. Your hair is therefore a symbol of your respect for the Feminine."

The missionaries command me to collect the tattered tufts of hair on either side of the chair and to put them in the burlap sack. I must also bury my moccasins and my clothes inside. The men dressed in black lead me to the yard behind the building. In the company of other children who've just suffered the same fate as me, I must make my way to a metal drum. A fire roars inside. One by one, we're forced to throw our bags into the flames. I witness the clothes that Mom so lovingly made me go up in smoke. I would later learn that a similar fate awaited my sisters on the other side of the wall that separated us. They too were forced to burn their clothes. Their beautiful hair was clipped high above their napes, leaving nothing but a pitiful bowl-cut crown.

After watching my hair and clothes burn to ashes, I'm led to the communal showers. We, who've been raised to respect the body and its privacy, now find ourselves brutally plunged into the most sordid of worlds. Young boys march out of the showers one by one, horrified. Tears roll down their cheeks in silence, for fear and shock have stifled their voices. I will soon learn why: three religious men await us in the showers, and they too are completely naked. Under the pretext of showing us how to wash ourselves, they use us to satisfy their sick sexual urges. Nowadays, I can put words to the thing. However, at eight years old, I'm defenceless and I know practically nothing about sexuality apart from what nature has taught me. One thing's certain: these men are doing us harm—and we understand full well that a great wrong is being perpetrated.

I would learn many years later that the same thing was happening to the little girls on the other side of the wall. The virus of sexual deviance, regrettably, had also corrupted some of the women of God who were tasked with caring for us.

This inconceivable reality would be the lot of 150 000 First Nations and Inuit children across Canada. In accordance with the *Gradual Civilization Act*, the Canadian government had granted itself the right to commit cultural genocide, some say. Others contend it committed genocide, plain and simple. Indeed, shortly before the amendment to the *Indian Act* became law in 1920, Duncan Campbell Scott, the most important high-ranking official in the Department of Indian Affairs, stated the following before a Special Committee of the House of Commons:

> I want to get rid of the Indian problem. I do not think as a matter of fact, that this country ought to continuously protect a class of people who are able to stand alone. That is my whole point... Our object is to continue until there is not a single Indian in Canada that has not been absorbed into the body politic, and there is no Indian question, and no Indian department, that is the whole object of this Bill. (National Archives of Canada 1920)

From the end of the nineteenth century onward, religious communities were allotted funds to take charge of the education of Indigenous youths aged five and up. The very last residential school closed its doors in 1996, in Saskatchewan.

After many years of silence, residential school survivors have now begun to speak up about their past. It's stupefying to discover how similar these testimonies are, irrespective of whether they concern residential schools in Western or Eastern Canada, or whether they were Catholic or Protestant establishments.

I don't know if Saint-Marc-de-Figuery was worse than other schools, but I can attest that from the first day we set foot on its grounds, the 250 boys and 250 girls who had been entrusted to the Church became victims of widespread physical, psychological, and sexual violence. It was our welcome present.

❖

To be sure, our everyday lives were punctuated by recesses and recreation periods, and yet I'm unable to recall any moments of true happiness or lightheartedness. The general atmosphere of the six years I spent inside those concrete walls was a grim one, perpetually characterized by fear and deep sorrow.

Three times a week, our days began with Mass. We were woken up at five thirty, attended a liturgical celebration in the chapel, and then ate breakfast. On the other mornings, we exercised in the yard or played hockey in the colder months. We were in class mornings and afternoons, studying French, mathematics, geography, history, and, of course, catechism. We would politely take our seats—boys on one side and girls on the other—at our numbered desks.

In fact, when we first arrived at the residential school, we were assigned a number that stayed with us until the end of our studies. Each and every article of clothing and all school supplies allotted to us bore this number—from our desks to our beds, our linen, our pencils and notebooks, and even our erasers. Not to mention our very person! For a reason I still can't grasp, the missionaries actually took to calling us by our numbers rather than our names. And yet, their own peers were the ones who had baptized us and given us Christian names! I suppose they gave us a number for practical reasons. Mine was 47.

"Forty-seven, what is God's First Commandment?"

"Fifty-three, what's four plus four?"

"Thirty-eight, conjugate the verb 'Have' in the imperfect tense."

I can still remember the names and numbers of each of my classmates. They're etched into my memory: 46, my brother Willy; 49, André Wylde; 51, Mathieu McDougall; 54, Maurice Kistabish, and so on.

The only time we were able to be near our sisters was during proper school hours. However, we couldn't talk to them because we weren't allowed to speak in class. In any case, during our first months at the school, we simply didn't *have* the words. We could only make out the girls' moods through their smiles or their tears. Until we could understand and speak a little French, we were condemned to silence, for the use of our own language was strictly prohibited. If we were caught speaking it, we were subjected to a series of punishments. When you see your friend getting his mouth washed out with soap or bleach, you quickly resolve that it's not worth the risk. "If you keep speaking your foul tongue," our schoolmasters would tell us repeatedly, "we'll cut it out!" This warning terrified me every time I heard it. From the perspective of an eight-year-old, the missionaries seemed quite capable of following through with their threats.

Learning French wasn't a smooth process. As a consequence of being repeatedly rapped over the fingers with a ruler or smacked behind the head, we gradually managed to absorb the *8emitekoci* vocabulary, and, as best we could, to interpret the concepts that accompanied their expressions. The one we called *tibiki kisis*—the night sun—or more affectionately *Kokom*—the Grandmother—simply became "the moon." *Oteimin* was no longer the fruit in the shape of a heart, but rather "the strawberry." *Onako*, which referred to something in the past, was no longer sufficient—from now on, we had to understand the nuances between yesterday, the other day, and last year. For us, the past is the past. It's hardly important, because what truly matters is every moment that's being lived *now*.

We also had to learn to address certain individuals by the familiar form and others by the formal form, according to certain social rules that often seemed quite arbitrary. To say nothing of French noun genders! The head (*la tête*) is feminine—even for a man!—but not the skull (*le crâne*) . . . We say "*le miel*" (the honey—masculine) and "*la confiture*" (the jam—feminine) . . . "*Une rivière*" (a river—feminine) and "*un ruisseau*" (a creek—masculine) . . . When I call *Mahikan* by name, I remain connected to its spirit. When I say *the* wolf, it's as if the article "the" distances me from the one I'm addressing . . . Maybe I didn't get enough raps over the fingers—or too many? The fact is that despite all their efforts, the *mekateokonek*[i] weren't able to mould my brain enough for it to either master French grammar or to share white people's outlook on life. To white people I say: *mik8etc* for sharing your language with me so that I, in turn, may better converse with you. But to dream by night, and to communicate by day, the Anicinape language will always be the one I'm most comfortable with.

As I mentioned at the beginning of this book, catechism lessons had a particularly disconcerting effect on me. For a long time, I believed in Heaven and Hell as they had been taught to us in school. During my

i The Black Robes.

childhood, I especially feared the Devil, who was talked about abundantly. If we didn't behave, we'd one day find ourselves with horns growing out of our heads, or so our teachers would have us believe. For quite some time, I was troubled by a group photo the missionaries had taken. On either side of my forehead, one could discern reflections that seemed to form two mysterious spots. I was convinced that these marks heralded the impending appearance of my horns. To make matters worse, this infernal photo was framed in the hallway. Whenever we walked past it, my classmates would take wicked pleasure in reminding me that my horns were on the verge of growing out!

The brainwashing process we were subjected to would become more confusing whenever the missionaries spoke to us about white people, who, according to them, were all sinners. Their depraved lives would lead them straight to Hell, while we, the lambs of the residential school, were sure to go to Heaven—as long as we stayed true to God's Commandments, of course. "White people are the Savages," they'd assure us. "You must not speak to them. Your parents too are Savages. They're filthy, and they don't know the good Lord. As for those who do not confess their sins, or—worse!—who have not received the sacrament of baptism, they are utterly doomed!"

In the philosophy of my ancestors, sin and punishment are unknown concepts. For us, human beings are all children of the Earth and of Creator, regardless of how they behave or where they come from. My people's children followed their Elders of their own accord in order to slowly learn their future adult roles. If they misbehaved, they'd be sent away in a canoe or into the woods to reflect on their conduct. As for the grown-ups, whenever they wished to express a concern or clear up a misunderstanding, they'd gather in a circle around the fire and discuss the matter. We were so powerfully animated by a spirit of tolerance and reconciliation that we didn't need Commandments to follow or punishments to make amends for our wrongdoings. The power of dissuasion has no place among a people who holds that there are no crimes—only missteps—a people who believes that every individual is responsible for their own growth via the teachings that are placed on their path.

Our Elders back home always preferred teaching harmony rather than how to maintain order. They fostered dialogue rather than the concept of law. In our tradition, every individual has freedom, but with that freedom comes the responsibility to speak. This teaches us to think for and by ourselves, and naturally incites us to get involved in the community. Our role isn't passive, as it is in societies where citizens must merely comply with a string of different codes of conduct in order to function. As a consequence of acting under the influence of fear, humans who blindly obey laws and rules become a little like robots. They might protest every now and then, but they tend to play their roles until there is little left of their humanity, to the point where they lose all interest in caring for the common good, Mother Earth, and all her inhabitants.

At the end of the eighteenth century, on the topic of the civilized world of white people versus the world of Savages, the famed Six Nations Mohawk Chief Joseph Brant was asked the following question: "Is civilization favourable to human happiness?" He answered thus:

> In the government you call civilized, the happiness of the people is constantly sacrificed to the splendor of empire. Hence your codes of criminal and civil laws have had their origin; hence your dungeons and prisons. I will not enlarge on an idea so singular in civilized life, and perhaps disagreeable to you, and will only observe, that among us we have *no* prisons.
> (Stone 1851, 481)

For us children who had never known violence, the residential school was shocking in all respects. We had to adapt to so many things in so little time! The question of our diet, for instance, was one of them. I come from the great Algonquian family. Since the dawn of time, we had picked, gathered, fished, hunted, and trapped what we needed to feed ourselves. Our diet was therefore almost exclusively based on meat and fish. In the summertime, we'd eat our fill of the berries Creator placed along our path, but growing vegetables and grains was not part of our lifestyle. Our bodies didn't require vegetables because it had always been that way. Everything we needed to be healthy, we could find in the forest. It goes without saying that we've had a hard time dealing with the processed foods that have appeared over the last few decades. Upon finding ourselves seated squarely and upright in the school dining hall, and served these strange meals, I must say that our hunger wasn't always accompanied by appetite. "What *is* this stuff?" I would ask myself, staring into my bowl of gruel. "It looks like the mush Mom and Dad used to prepare for the dogs. But now, *I'm* the one who has to swallow down the disgusting slop, whether I want to or not." Back home, we only ate when we were hungry. There was always some kind of food ready to be served at the camp, and we didn't have our meals at fixed hours. The missionaries, on the other hand, made us eat three times a day and forced us to finish our plates, regardless of how full we were. Once again, we learned this the hard way—after witnessing our more stubborn friends have their faces ungraciously pressed into their pea soup or their mashed potatoes by an iron-fisted religious Brother or Sister.

Our days at school were fixed like clockwork, divided into prayers, meals, studies, and recess. The hour we dreaded the most was bedtime. After supper we'd get to play checkers, snakes and ladders, dodgeball, or hockey for a short while before the Brothers signalled that it was time to go up to the dormitory. Like good little soldiers we'd form ranks, climb the stairs, and take a seat on our beds until our numbers were called to proceed to the washroom one by one. We'd wash up and put on our pajamas in front of these black-robed men, whose invasive gazes left us constantly feeling unclean despite our best scrubbing efforts. These nightly rituals had to be performed in perfect silence, or else we'd risk getting the stick.

During our first days at the residential school, one boy among us had learned that we shouldn't take the Brothers' threats lightly. He had merely dared to speak in the ranks. In a characteristic fit of rage, Brother Boivin[i] suddenly grabbed him by the neck to give him a smack. He forced him to kneel near the stairwell, and while shouting his orders, struck him so hard that our classmate's forehead rammed violently against the wall corner and started gushing blood. We were quickly asked to clean up the mess, and this first scene of extreme violence at the school haunted me for a long time. In the ranks, I was always as quiet as the grave.

After the boys were sound asleep in their beds, the three night lurkers would make their appearance. Brother Boivin, Brother Grenier, and Brother Ménard were tasked, among other things, with supervising the dormitories. For this reason, their cells were right next to the large room where we were meant to have "sweet dreams." The first time they came for me, I was still eight years old. It was late at night. The other children were deep in slumber when Brother Boivin suddenly roused me awake:

"Forty-seven, wake up," he whispered, so as not to wake the others. "We need you to help fold linens in the laundry room."

Wary, but far from imagining what was to come, I rubbed my eyes and followed Brother Boivin to the basement. I would later learn that the laundry room was one of the most dangerous places in the residential school, ranked after the three night lurkers' cells, the showers, and the confessional, not to mention the storeroom we would later dub the "room of martyrs"—a grim chamber in which we suffered many torments at the hands of the Brothers. On the walls of this dark cellar hung their instruments of torture: horse straps and belts of all sizes, sawed-off hockey sticks, baseball bats, and more. The Brothers even had a bench vise with rubber-lined jaws. They sometimes used it to crush our hands until we confessed the "truth." I remember having seen, time and time again, students leave the room of martyrs with bloodied fingers and shattered nails.

i We have withheld the real names of the perpetrators.

❖

Brother Grenier was waiting for us when we reached the laundry room. While he showed me how to fold the towels and sheets piled before us, Brother Boivin started caressing my back, and then my buttocks. That's when I realized I'd fallen into a trap. I struggled, but the two men forced me to remove my pajamas. Even though they were much stronger than I was, I miraculously managed to escape their clutches. Stark naked, I ran upstairs to the classrooms floor. Brother Boivin and Brother Grenier searched for me in the darkness. After hiding in a classroom, I scurried to the washroom and entered one of the many stalls. Just as one of my stalkers walked in, I climbed onto the toilet bowl so that he couldn't see my feet under the door. The missionary turned on the lights, and believing no one was there, turned them off again and left. My heart was pounding. I waited a while, and then had the idea of heading to the older boys' dormitory to seek refuge in my brother Willy's bed. I was lucky—no one saw me. I managed to find my big brother and slid under the blankets. Willy awoke with a start:

"Dominique? What's going on? What are you doing here, naked in the middle of the night? Where are your pajamas?"

"They're in the laundry room. Brother Boivin and Brother Grenier asked me to help them fold some laundry . . ."

I didn't have to say any more—Willy knew the rest. Sooner or later, everyone found out about the twisted conduct of these three religious Brothers, the very men who were entrusted with guarding us while we slept. All of a sudden, Brother Boivin materialized in the doorway and made his way to the foot of the bed. Evidently, he guessed that I would seek out my elder brother. Handing me new pajamas, the clever liar addressed me in a deceptively reassuring voice: "There you are, 47! We looked for you everywhere, you know. Here, put these pajamas on and go back to bed." Then, turning to Willy, he said: "Don't worry about your brother. He simply had what we call a sleepwalking episode. He took off his clothes and walked all the way here in his sleep."

❖

I couldn't sleep a wink the rest of the night. I was too afraid that one of the Brothers might come back for me. It seems, however, that my gutsiness had subdued their zeal, because they left me alone. The following morning, I found candies in my locker—a gift from my two abusers. It was their way of buying my silence. I shared them with my friends. Even though we loved sweets, those that would discreetly find their way into our hands during our time at the school always had a bitter aftertaste, it seemed, for we understood their true price.

On another note, I should add that we were always hungry back then. On top of not being particularly appetizing, our rations were rather meagre, and our desserts, quite rare. As the years went by, we took some initiative and found out how to filch bread, jam, or cookies from the large pantry. We would regularly stock up on food and hide it in a secret crawlspace under a raised building. We simply had to put a few planks back in place before leaving, and you'd never have known it was there. It was a very good hideout, where we could snack and chitchat in peace for a short while. When we reappeared in the midst of the larger group, the missionaries were none the wiser!

The baker had also developed the habit of surreptitiously slipping us pastries when we helped him unload his bread crates, so you can imagine how we flocked to him whenever we saw his truck pull in. He was the only white layperson to enter the walls of our compound during our first years at the Saint-Marc residential school. This good and simple man was our one and only link to the outside world. After learning to write a little, we'd slip distress messages into his hand or his pocket, careful not to get caught by the missionaries. We implored him to act: "Please, give these messages to our parents. Tell them they're doing us harm here."

At the time, we were convinced the baker knew our parents and where they lived. We hadn't learned that, in order for a letter to be sent, one must know the recipient's address. But even if we'd understood how the post worked, we wouldn't have known how to find our parents, for they still camped here and there, at the whims of evictions and the odd jobs our fathers could find. The result, of course, was that none of our letters ever reached their destinations. What's more, back in those days, the law of silence not only reigned within the walls of the residential school, but also in all the Christian homes in the country. The Church's supremacy was so pervasive that none would have dared denounce a religious figure, much less an entire order. We even tried reporting the lurking Brothers to the head priest, but in vain. Every time we sought help from higher up, we were punished. Our poor baker must have felt quite powerless. I imagine all he could do to alleviate our suffering was to offer us these little clandestine sweets, and to pray for us.

❖

Nowadays, I no longer have chills of horror when I speak of the abuses I endured or witnessed. Occasionally, certain emotions resurface, but the anger and the sorrow have left my body and I now live in peace. That said, this written testimony forces me to stir up the past and revisit it. It's a delicate exercise, because I aspire to share a message of healing and I have the responsibility of communicating it to the best of my ability. How does one find the proper words to convey to a reader the gravity of the crimes that were committed, while simultaneously respecting the dignity of those involved? How does one testify against these sordid daily occurrences without slipping into voyeurism and without a vengeful spirit?

Thanks to the temperament that would one day make me a leader—which had manifested itself since my early childhood—I think that our aggressors spared me somewhat. They seemed to naturally focus on the frailer and more timid children. Despite this, I was no stranger to their brutality. Without going into detail, I can affirm that, when I was a child, my nights at the residential school were haunted by these pedophilic Brothers. Every night, they'd creep into our dormitories to indulge in their vices. One by one, sooner or later, we all had our turn. As for me—perhaps every two months. One of them would snatch me from my bed and take me to his cell. First, he'd pray, then he'd remove all his clothes and talk to me about God, the flesh, and his body, while inviting me to perform certain acts on his person or on my own.

Sometimes, a child would be dragged out into the woods. Sometimes, it happened in some dark corner of our building. The depravity of these religious figures even reached into the confessionals, where, after having listened to our sins, they would ask us to lower our pants and pray the Rosary as penitence, while they leered at us or masturbated on the other side of the lattice.

After many years of silence, some of my sisters also spoke up about the abuses they suffered on their side, at the hands of both men and women. Indeed, religious Sisters also participated in this great collective madness that befell residential schools in the times of the *Grande Noirceur*.

The first naked women I set my eyes upon were religious Sisters who were as twisted as our male jailers. One day, some Brothers had asked me and my cousin Mathieu to bring sandwiches to some Sisters who'd gone for a swim in the nearby lake. We were always glad and proud to be entrusted with a special task. Alas, once we arrived on the scene, our joy gave way to disenchantment. Yet again, we were asked to watch or perform things that should never be imposed on children anywhere on Earth.

Before I wrap up this part of my story, I want to note that although these crimes were not perpetuated by the whole of the teaching staff, violent acts of a moral, physical, or sexual nature were our daily lot—all of us children—and that there was sufficient complicity among the school's holy men and women to cause immeasurable ravages among our people, which are still very much felt several generations later. For the most part, these crimes will remain unpunished, and, as everyone now knows, secrecy remains stronger within the realm of the Church than in the realm of Truth. For the time being, at least . . .

On our first Christmas Eve at Saint-Marc-de-Figuery, we were surprised to learn that Mom and Dad were waiting for us in the reception parlour. My sister Cécile tells me that this visit took place four months after we arrived at the residential school, but in my mind, that period felt so interminable that it seemed like over a year had gone by before my parents first visited us in our prison. And so, all six of us were called down to spend a few minutes with them. Before opening the parlour door, the Brothers were quite explicit: "Behave and stay on your side of the room. You're not allowed to touch your parents, or to speak to them in your Savage tongue. You know what's coming to you if you choose not to speak French!"

Willy, my four sisters, and I entered the parlour. Our parents were waiting at the far end of the room. In the centre, a priest and a Sister supervised our reunion. We quivered at the sight of our parents, this man and woman we loved so much. My sisters sobbed in silence. My brother and I also shed a few tears, but we hid our emotions under a thin veneer of spite:

"Look at how filthy our parents are," declared my brother—in French.

"It's true. They *do* look like a couple of Savages!" I added, before sharing a muffled snicker with him. In truth, our nervousness, and most of all, the immense inner turmoil we felt, pushed us to utter these insults. Thankfully, my parents didn't hear. Mockery gave us the illusion of strength, and perhaps also hid our anger. At the time, we felt as though our parents had abandoned us.

My mother was taking it hard at the other end of the room. She spoke neither French nor English but she could read the suffering on our faces, and broke down into tears upon seeing our overall appearances:

"*8essa! Ecinakosi8atc ota apinotcicak!* Look at our children!" she exclaimed, turning to my father. "They've lost their hair and their tans! They look sick! We have to bring them home!"

"You know very well that it's impossible, Emma. It's against the law."

To see my mother in that state—crying and sensing our inner anguish—made me blow up. Too bad for the punishments that would follow. I had to speak up—to tell them what was happening in this damned school.

"*Tep8e, Dada!* It's true, Dad! Mom's right. They're hurting us! *Ni 8i ki8e nokom!* I want to go home now!"

The problem is that in our language, the word "rape" doesn't exist. I didn't have the means to communicate this incomprehensible concept to Anicinape adults of their generation. In any case, it was already too late. A Brother grabbed me by the collar and hauled me out of the parlour. He hurtled down the stairs dragging me by the ear (one day, in fact, I was dragged by the ear so violently that it left me with permanent hearing loss), and, upon reaching the great hall, ordered me to kneel down on a wooden rod:

"Stay there and don't move until you're told your penitence is over. That'll teach to you to speak your filthy language!"

I stayed there for several long minutes, in tremendous pain, not merely from my ruined knees but also from my child's heart, which felt lost and alone amid all these injustices. A while later, Willy appeared. "Mom and Dad are gone," he informed me. On the sly, he casually kicked the wooden stick from under my knees, sending it shuffling across the room, and left.

Shortly after, a missionary came to tell me my punishment was over. "And remember to be obedient next time," he chided as he picked me up by the arm. He didn't notice that the rod was over by the wall and never realized that Willy had helped me out of this unfortunate situation.

The following day, our parents and those of our classmates were invited to celebrate Midnight Mass with us. Once again, the missionaries listed the rules we were expected to follow to the letter:

"You must stay still and quiet during Mass. Your parents will be up in the *jubé*,[i] while you will stay in the *chœur*.[ii] Those who turn to look at their parents or wave to them will be punished and won't be allowed to see them after Mass. Understood?"

And so, we entered the chapel in an orderly line. We stood as straight as soldiers during the entire service, which felt like an eternity. I had to restrain myself with all my might to keep from turning toward my parents.

i The tribunes, or upper balconies.

ii The nave.

The wait was all the more intolerable whenever I managed to single out their voices during hymns. They sang *Minuit, chrétiens* (*O Holy Night*) and *Adeste Fideles* (*O Come, All Ye Faithful*) in Anicinape that night. Someday way back when, the missionaries had translated the lyrics for our people and found it charming to hear their flock sing the glory of God in the Indian tongue. And yet, we children of Saint-Marc had been taught to renounce our language entirely, whether it be in speech or in song. It was but one of the many contradictions of our reality. But for the moment, Mom and Dad were indeed here in the flesh, a few metres above me. I could recognize their beautiful voices, and soon, if I behaved, I would finally be able to see them during our small family Christmas gathering.

I must say that many religious figures at the school were excellent teachers and spiritual guides. I have very fond memories of most of the individuals who oversaw my education, men who were sincerely and fundamentally good, who taught us innumerable things that proved essential to surviving in the modern age. These true missionaries were the planners behind Christmas celebrations, carnivals, Olympiads, and team sports events, which have left me with happy memories. Sometimes on Saturday mornings, the Brothers would give us sandwiches and release us into the forest:

"Go on, go! Run off into the woods! Just make sure you're back by this afternoon!" For us, it was pure joy. An entire day to roam the area freely, in this forest that felt like home! Sometimes our parents were invited to celebrations, and in the days leading up to them, we were even allowed to set snares to catch hare or grouse. We'd return triumphantly with our quarries, and gave them to the Sisters. They would prepare them *their* way, but it was still pretty tasty.

When I was a little older, I was part of a small group of boys who loved to break the rules whenever the coast was clear. Weekend mornings were often reserved for a variety of odd jobs, such as shovelling snow, planting trees, or stacking firewood. The afternoons were for napping, and we'd take the opportunity to sneak away unnoticed. Unbeknownst to our guardians, we'd go skating on the frozen lake or tobogganing on the snowy slopes. No one could see us from the main building. On a handful of occasions, we'd make our way to the stable down the hill and free the cows. For us, keeping animals caged up was inconceivable. We were sometimes allowed to watch a little TV and had seen a few broadcasts of rodeos, so you can imagine the laugh we had one day when our friend Oscar decided to play cowboy and ride a cow. Other days, we'd be Robin Hood and his Merry Men, and swordfight with sawed-off hockey sticks. I still bear a scar on my chest—a vestige of a "sword" strike to the heart.

Among the diversions we were allowed to partake in, nothing could beat Canada's national sport, ice hockey, and its heroes—Maurice Richard, Jean Béliveau, "Boum-Boum" Geoffrion, and Claude Provost (my favourite player!). We were introduced to the rudiments of the sport by white people, starting with the art of standing up on skates. In fact, the eminent Serge Savard[i] was the one who laced up my skates for the very first time! Since hockey grew out of old Indigenous games, young Anicinapek picked up the sport quickly and many of them became excellent players. For us, hockey is second nature. It didn't take me long to become a good skater, a good scorer, and . . . a good fighter!

I started playing against white teams at the age of ten or eleven. The regional clubs would come by the residential school on weekends to challenge us. We also got the chance to play in tournaments elsewhere in the province as far as Quebec City! The stronger we got over the years, the more aggressive we became, owing to the awful secrets of our lives at the school. In our early teens, my teammates and I started taking pleasure in giving white kids a good clobbering during our hockey matches. We'd check them hard against the boards and had become masters at jabbing them in the ribs with the butt end of our sticks at every opportunity. We called these "six-inchers" (hockey players will know what I'm talking about!), and our adversaries would instantly fall to the ice, hollering

i A former defenceman for the Montreal Canadiens (the glorious NHL team!), Serge Savard was born in 1946 in Landrienne, Abitibi.

contemptuously: "You damn Savages!" These insults provided us yet another pretext to go on brawling.

I can still remember how I once caught the end of a stick right in the mouth, curtesy of a vengeful white boy who'd been on the receiving end of my blows since the beginning of the game. The result: I'm still missing two molars. The height of absurdity was that whenever a white player cursed us ("*Tabarnak!* You dirty son-of-a-bitch! . . . *Ostie!* Just wait until I get my hands on you, you goddamn Savage!!"),[i] we'd play the nice innocent lambs once we were back on the bench and tell the missionaries: "You see number 8, over there? Well, he just blasphemed. Same goes for number 22!" So, between the periods, we'd kneel with the missionaries and pray for the young white players—the real Savages, according to our tutors—so that they wouldn't end up in Hell for their trespasses!

The return of warmer weather would always announce our homecoming. I remember well the very first time Dad came to pick us up at the end of the school year. Since he didn't own a vehicle (and First Nations were still not allowed to use public transit), he had asked our neighbour in Amos, Mr. Jean-Paul Ouellet, to be our chauffeur. I can still picture the six of us climbing into his huge car and driving away, back on the road to freedom. What a joy it was to return to the family nest, to finally be able to play with our brothers and sisters, to wear the clothes we wanted to wear, to rediscover the aromas and flavours of Mom's cooking: beaver meat, goose, or a big old pike. What a treat!

During our first few summer vacations, we were glad to be able to speak our language freely again. But as the years went by, we drifted further and further from our culture. Many of us became more and more comfortable speaking French, either out of fear of reprisal, or out of a desire to live a more modern life among white people and to better fit in with the masses.

---

i While Québécois French expletives are difficult to translate directly, suffice it to say that they are often derived from liturgical terms, and are therefore flagrantly blasphemous.

It would always take us some time to find our footing again when we got home. We had missed our family so much that we didn't dare leave it. We felt a fervent need to stay close to our mom and dad. However, we didn't have the strength to breathe a word about the awful things that were routinely taking place back at the residential school. I think that each of us was perhaps too happy to rediscover the familiar and too busy making the best of our sacred moments together.

As for me, my father picked up wherever we had left off and took me with him on extraordinary adventures in the forest, or to meet Medicine Men and Women. It was all part of my training as an apprentice. In spite of my residential school experience, our Elders maintained that I was different from other children—that I had to be protected and trained in secret. Whenever they had the chance, they would teach me what I needed to know as future *Okima*. They spoke regularly about the day when I would feel ready to tackle my role of young Medicine Man and seek out the "Spirit of the Forest."

Among the Elders Dad liked me to spend time with was *Tcomitc* Black. Grandfather Black belonged to the Bear Clan and would spend his summers at Low Bush, on the Ontarian side of Lake Abitibi. I was always enormously impressed with his teachings and his astonishing stories about *Manto Mak8a*,[i] the Spirit of the Bear. Every spring, he would gather the orphaned bear cubs he found in the forest and nurse them until they were old enough to be released back into the wild. Whenever Dad and I would reach his home, he'd always ask me: "*Aca na kikinta8ama ki Mak8a?* So? Have you met your bear yet?"

When I was young, this question frightened me. I felt as though I was absolutely incapable of living through such an experience. And yet, I knew full well that the Spirit of the Bear and my own were connected in a special way. How many times had the Bear visited me in my dreams? Sometimes, we'd take a stroll together or tussle or even go for a swim in a beautiful lake. These dreams never scared me, for the Bear was always amicable and protective. When I'd wake up, I'd share these dreams with

i Pronounced "Man-doo Mah-koo-ah."

my mother, who too predicted than one of these days, the Bear would cross my path.

And so, in my twelfth summer, I felt ready to prove my worth. I had grown, and I knew that I was up to the task—that I could show my parents that I had committed to memory everything they had taught me about survival over the years. For us, a child gradually enters adulthood around the age of twelve. Summer was coming to an end, the nights were still warm, and the forest abounded with all kinds of good things to nourish us. One fine morning, with a mix of confidence, boldness, and a touch of pride, I told my father that I felt I was ready to undergo this first initiation and seek out the Spirit of the Forest. In my case, it was evident that this would be the Spirit of the Bear. Once I found him, I knew that he would thereafter accompany and assist me throughout my life as a Medicine Man.

"Really? You've decided?" my father asked, looking at me straight in the eye.

"Yes. I'm ready to leave home."

"All right. I'll start preparing for our travels."

At the time of my big announcement, we were at our big house in Amos. But as far as Traditional Medicine was concerned, everything we did happened in the 8akocik River area, west of Lake Abitibi. That was where my first initiation would take place.

After preparing for a few days, my father, my mother, and I left for 8akocik. The rest of my family was unaware of our expedition's true purpose, since my parents didn't want to place their children in a precarious situation with the authorities.

Upon reaching 8akocik, Dad told me that everything was set for my initiation. Night fell, and, next to the fire, we went over everything pertaining to the trial:

"Now, you can leave and go into the forest. I'll accompany you by canoe to where you'll be staying until the Spirit seeks you out. You'll be staying there for as long as you have to. You remember how to build your trap to catch the Spirit?"

"Yes, Dad."

"If the Spirit refuses to enter your trap, or if you harm it and it flees, you'll fail the test. Understood?"

"*Ehe*. Yes."

"You haven't forgotten what to do to light your Sacred Fire, even if it rains?"

"*Ka8in*. No."

"At night, you might feel lonelier than when the sun's out. Think of it as if you were inside your mother's belly, enveloped and protected by the darkness. You should never be afraid of it."

My father paused. The fire shimmered before us. The forest was calm. Dad spoke again, finishing our review:

"We've taught you everything, Kapiteotak. It's up to you now to show us that you know how to live alone in the forest, like a man. Since you say you're ready, you'll leave tomorrow at dawn."

This caught me off-guard—I hadn't expected things to move along so quickly. "Tomorrow morning?" I thought. "That's too soon!" Confronted so abruptly with the imminence of my departure, I wasn't feeling so sure of myself anymore. I grew more and more agitated as the hours passed. Dawn must not have been far off by the time I fell asleep. When I opened my eyes, Mom was packing a large backpack, but Dad wasn't in the tent.

"*Ati Dada?* Where's Dad?"

"He's by the river," answered Mom. "He's getting the canoe ready for our departure. I decided to tag along to see you off. *Ki 8i 8isin na?* Are you hungry?"

"*Ehe*."

"Here, eat well," she said, handing me a bowl of hare soup, our favourite dish.

I ate my soup with gusto and my father walked in as my mother was finishing up packing my bag.

“*K8e, Kapiteotak! Ki mino matisin na?* Good morning, Kapiteotak! You’re feeling well?”

“*Ehe*, but I didn’t sleep much.”

“You’re a good warrior, my son. All will be well,” answered my father in a firm but reassuring tone.

Then, pointing at the bag my mother had just prepared, he asked her: “What’s this? What did you put in that bag?”

“Well, it’s everything he’ll need—a blanket, a change of clothes, a knife, a bit of food, and matches.”

“No! Kapiteotak knows how to survive in the forest without any of that. The bag will stay here,” decreed my father. “*A8sa, macatan!* Now, let’s go!”

With the slightest twinge in my heart, I take my seat at the centre of the canoe. Mom settles in at the bow and Dad sits behind me. Mom pushes us away from the bank with her paddle, and the canoe slides smoothly off the sand and onto the river. We start paddling together, but without haste. Every stroke is slow and precise. The trick is to find a good cruising rhythm without overly exerting ourselves, and most of all, to be in perfect harmony with the water and the other elements that surround us. *Tciman*, the canoe, isn’t merely an object to us. To travel in one is truly like meditating. *Tciman* is Medicine.

And so, we progress, gliding delicately on the river, which is like a mirror on this calm August morning. Now and then, families of ducks take flight as we approach them. The Canadian forest is wholly submerged in its characteristic magnificent silence. Dad is humming, and with his every stroke you can hear the drops trickle softly down his paddle and return to the river. From the front of the canoe comes another kind of song—Mom can no longer hold back her tears. I thought I had detected some emotion in her a little earlier, when she hugged me before we left. Now that we can’t see her face, she’s allowing herself to cry. I can understand why she’s emotional—her little boy is about to become a man.

We travel many kilometres on the 8akocik River without stopping. After several hours, my father tells us that we're nearing my destination. Before we reach the shore, Dad suggests that I reconnoitre around the site as soon as we disembark.

"I want you to explore the surroundings," he says. "Then I want you to tell me the names of all the trees and plants that can lend you their Medicine during your stay. Understood?"

He gives the canoe a final thrust with his usual dexterity and the tip of the craft slides gently onto a small beach of fine sand. Mom gets out first, without getting her toes wet, and she hauls the canoe ashore so that we too can regain dry land.

Once we're on the bank, we stretch our legs and take a good look around. We drink some water, and Dad suggests I get started right away: "Take note of all the Medicine around you and then report back to me." Glad for the opportunity to show my father the fruits of my training, I head into the woods at once. After a good ten minutes or so, I've located blueberries, fir, spruce, cedar, birch, and a number of other plants that will play an important role in my survival exercise. I enthusiastically make my way back to our little beach, but the canoe's no longer there. Yet, I'm sure that this is the right place. Yes, it's definitely the same beach. I scan the horizon and to my great dismay, I discern my parents in the distance, already making their way back to camp. The canoe's racing down the river, irrevocably pulling away from me. I can see them rounding the point way out there, and finally disappear—never once looking back in my direction. I'm aghast. "They took off without so much as a kiss or a hug!" I find myself thinking. "They left me here and didn't even take the time to say goodbye! But why? . . . Why?"

Their sudden departure and the weight of my solitude hit me like a ton of bricks—it's as if the whole sky has come crashing down onto my head. In an instant, I process the magnitude of my trial, and then panic grabs hold of me. I collapse in tears at the foot of a tree. My parents, my grandparents and the other Elders, my brothers and sisters, my uncles and aunts, my cousins, our dogs—everyone I care for is absent. No one to keep me company. I've never felt so alone. I'll never get through it! I cry until I run out of tears and find that I no longer have the energy to feed my anguish. My body shudders as a few final sobs escape me, but, as I wipe my nose with my sleeve, my head is clearing. Just as though I'm watching a movie, I can suddenly see and hear the Elders showing me what to do when one sets up a new camp—first, I must light my Sacred Fire, which I won't allow to burn out for the duration of my test, then I must build a shelter, and finally, I must search for food. My father's words echo in my spirit: "Give yourself everything. In the forest, never let yourself be in want of anything."

Propelled by a newfound strength, I start by gathering dry firewood. There's plenty in the area. I proceed to kindle the fire without a lighter or matches. Like the Elders taught me, I first arrange some twigs on a bone-dry cedar branch. Amid the twigs, I place very fine pieces of birch bark, and I position my cedar spindle vertically onto the centre of the bundle. I spin the stick between my palms repeatedly, and soon, the friction has created enough heat to ignite the bark and the twigs. At the heart of my very first solo camp, my Sacred Fire has been lit.

Once my fire is fed and burning well, I build a reflector wall on one side of it, and on the other, my lean-to shelter—fashioned with two large Y-shaped branches for poles and three others to complete the frame. Big bushy fir branches complete the roof, and finer ones will make for a comfortable and fragrant mattress. "Remember to leave a ventilation hole in your survival shelter," my dad's voice reminds me. "With the reflector wall facing you, this vent will suck in warm air. This way, you'll never be cold inside your refuge, even in the winter."

My lean-to is now set up and I'm quite proud of my handiwork. It's time to go pick those blueberries I saw earlier, a few minutes' walk from the beach. Soon, evening falls, and having eaten my fill of succulent fruit, I effortlessly fall asleep on my fir-branch mattress, comforted by my Sacred Fire.

The following day unfolds without a hitch. I gather firewood, find more blueberry bushes, and even successfully track down a grouse. I ask it if it agrees to offer me its life, just like I learned from the Elders, and I throw a sturdy stick in its direction, aiming for the head. When I approach the bird, I see that it's given itself to me. For us, it's essential to pray as we hunt, and we try to avoid inflicting undue suffering and causing unnecessary bloodshed. The little grouse agreed to my prayer. I roast the bird on the end of a stick over the embers, and, as my father counselled, eat only half, leaving the rest as an offering to the Spirit I came to seek out.

Tonight seems to drag on longer than yesterday evening, and now that my camp's properly set up and I have things to eat, I'm a little bored. I decide to go to bed early—tomorrow, I'll explore some more. Who knows?—maybe I'll stumble upon bear tracks. With all the blueberries around here, I wouldn't be surprised.

I'm dozing serenely in my shelter when night falls, but my rest is interrupted by a noise in the nearby bushes. I'm sure it's an animal. I can hear it snorting and shuffling back and forth out there, behind the fire. Is it a fox? A wolf? I can't tell in the shadows. I decide to feed the fire in the hope of getting better light. While applying myself to this task, the Spirit pounces out of the darkness without warning and makes itself known to me in all its splendour: *Mak8a*—the Bear—is here in the flesh, a few metres away, and by all appearances, in quite a bad mood. Clearly, my presence on his territory has upset him. The bear shifts backwards, stands tall on his hind legs, and throws a growl of discontent my way before bolting back into the woods the way he came. My heart's beating hard and fast, and I add wood to the fire, knowing that *Mak8a* won't dare approach the flames. Still, I reach for my long walking stick. I also know that one can defend oneself by keeping such a tool pointed toward an animal's snout. It gives it the impression that the wielder becomes larger, which scares and confuses the animal. It's an excellent trick and nobody gets hurt.

After a few minutes have elapsed, my friend returns in a huff. Since I was expecting him, he leaves me be—I'm too close to the fire. Instead, he goes after my shelter. With a few swipes of his paws, he sends the fir branches scattering through the air, and the lean-to frame collapses. Once again he stands on his hind legs, displaying his anger to me, and flees into the forest. For a good while I just sit there immobile, shaken by this magnificent animal's demonstration of force. I must say, for our first encounter, *Mak8a* was decidedly unceremonious!

The bear seems to have opted to leave me alone for the time being, and now that the silence of the night envelops me again, the teachings of the Beaver come back to me. What do beavers do when one destroys their dams or their lodges? They rebuild everything immediately, without dithering. With the Beaver's resolution, I put everything back in place. In less than an hour, I'm back in my warm shelter. Exhausted from this emotional ordeal, I sink into slumber and sleep like the dead.

I sleep in the next morning and the day goes by slowly, punctuated by my harvesting of nutritious roots, blueberry picking, and the gathering of firewood, which I now have to seek out farther and farther away. Every morning, I take the time to pray at daybreak and to make my Cedar offerings to thank Creator for all the Medicine and the food He has placed on my path.

I'm by my Sacred Fire singing softly when night falls. All of a sudden —a noise in the bushes! Grunting! *Mak8a* has returned!

"*Manto Mak8a*, be calm," I tell him in my language. "I'd like to be your friend. I came here to meet you and to ask . . ."

Mak8a couldn't care less about my reasons. Like yesterday, he flies into a rage. While I take refuge by the fire, he rushes onto my shelter and unleashes his anger. He's furious, and my words don't seem to have any effect. Once again, he escapes and doesn't return for the rest of the night. And I, following the Beaver's example, patiently rebuild my shelter.

The next evening, the bear returns to deliver his message a third time, repeating exactly the same routine. And I clean up after him. It's a little game we play, he and I.

However, the night after that, *Mak8a*'s nowhere to be seen. No scene of destruction, no fit of anger, no noise in the bushes. Nothing. Strangely, the night seems longer than usual. Nothing of note happens the next day either. To be honest, even though he was quite menacing, I was starting to appreciate my new friend's nightly visits. In his own way, he was spicing up my solitary stay. Now I have no one to keep me company, and as the day drags on, doubt creeps into my spirit. Maybe I went about it the wrong way with *Mak8a*. Maybe I made him go away for good. Maybe I should have set up my trap long ago and asked him for his life right away. Have I failed my test?

These increasingly pressing worries occupy my thoughts as I find my sleep on the fifth night of my initiation to becoming a Medicine Man. Still, night brings good counsel, and by morning my mind has cleared a little. While I fill my belly with the small edible plants that grow near my encampment, it occurs to me that *Mak8a* visits me at night because he sleeps during the day. When I was very young, I was taught that one must always be wary of mother bears, who can become aggressive if one inadvertently comes between her and her cubs. In this case, however, I'm dealing with a young male. If my presence here riles him up so much, it must be because I'm near his den. And so, that very morning I decide to go and seek him out, now convinced that the Spirit can't be very far.

Taking note of the broken branches he's left behind, I quickly find his tracks. After a few minutes, I discover what might very well be the entrance to his lair. Under a rocky mound, an opening seems to lead to a wider and deeper cave. What's more, in the dirt, I notice a number of tracks coming and going, as well as a distinctive odour emanating from within. There's no doubt that a wild animal lives here, but is it my bear? My intuition tells me that it is, but how can I be certain? Then, I remember our little game, and come up with the idea to pick it up where we left off. When *Mak8a* visited me, he liked messing up my shelter. Why then shouldn't I do the same? Since the number seven is esteemed in our tradition, I align seven round stones in front of his doorway. I wind back my leg and with a kick, send the first stone flying into the lair. I hear it roll and then settle to a stop at the back of the cavity. I keep it up: two, three, four . . . With the fifth stone, I hit my target. I hear a grunt and I recognize my bear. Quickly, I send the remaining stones careening into the darkness before turning away and beating a hasty retreat. I turn to look back behind me a few times, but I see nothing. Out of breath, I find my camp, and proceed to throw logs onto my fire with no little urgency. But all remains calm. The Spirit hasn't followed me.

It's now the seventh day of my initiation. The night was uneventful and I slept well. Once the sun has climbed over the mountains, I start making my way back to the lair. I look forward to meeting *Mak8a*—with each passing day I'm more and more in communion with him. I speak to him from afar and pray: "*Manto*, I offer you the opportunity to become my support and my principal Medicine for the rest of my days. If this is your wish and that of the Great Spirit, give me your life. In exchange for it, I promise to always be true to you."

At last I reach the den. Imagine my surprise at finding all seven of my stones back outside the cave! *Mak8a* rolled them out one by one! Like me (or like the Beaver!), he has patiently repaired his home. Since my friend demolished my shelter on three occasions, I'll do the same. And so, I send the stones back inside, and repeat the process the next day.

On the eighth day of my initiation, I feel that the time has come to act. After carrying out the seven-stone drill once more, I place some Cedar in front of the entrance one last time, and ask the bear for his life: "*Manto*, I'm now ready to prepare my trap. If you've agreed to become my Medicine Spirit, I'm waiting for you. If you choose not to visit my trap, I'll abide by your decision."

I quickly get to work and begin setting up the trap, just the way my father taught me. I place a tree trunk on the ground and above it, position three more sloped logs piggybacked on one another, whose raised ends are simply held up by a sturdy stick. A thin, long root connects this stick to bait. Over my several meetings with *Mak8a*, I made sure to observe him well and estimate the length of his paws. This detail is essential to building this kind of trap. When a bear engages with such a contraption, it reaches for the bait with an outstretched paw—it never sticks its entire body inside. With this in mind, I build my trap accounting for his size. Then, I set the bait—the uneaten half of that grouse I caught the other day. When the Spirit grabs hold of the bait, it'll set off the trap. The upper logs will come crashing down onto his back and will crush his thorax against the lower trunk. Death will be instantaneous, as it should be, without suffering or bloodshed. Lastly, I cover my trap with fir branches on all sides but the opening, and, after a final prayer, I return to my camp.

It's my ninth morning. Day has broken and I'm eager to find out whether *Mak8a* has agreed to become my companion in life. My heart thumps wildly as I walk toward the trap near the lair. When I arrive, I stop dead in my tracks, amazed. I don't dare believe it—between the collapsed logs of my trap lies the immobile body of a bear. I approach it slowly, and behold its head inside. The Spirit's eyes are open and the glassy gaze confirms that he has agreed to bind himself to my life! I sit on a rock and contemplate the scene for a long time. It's not the first time I'm faced with the death of an animal. It's part of any young Anicinape hunter's upbringing. Nevertheless, even though a bear can offer us its meat, we often choose to do without it—we very rarely kill bears, for we hold this Spirit in the highest regard. In any case, bit by bit, it dawns on me that I've passed my test. I'm moved to know that the Spirit has accepted my proposed alliance. I'm even more moved when I think about the consequences of my success. The die has been cast: I've become a man, I'm following in the footsteps of my predecessors, and have taken a great leap forward on the path of Medicine.

At length, I give my thanks to *Mak8a* and the inestimable boon he has given me. I set down Cedar all around his body, and I carefully collect two claws that I'll take with me—one for Dad, and the other for Mom.

I return to my campsite to clean up and to snuff out my fire, and then, I start my journey home. The trial's over and it's time to find my parents to tell them the big news. Light-hearted and light-footed, I set a course for their camp. I'm only twelve, but by now I can find my way in the forest with ease. I no longer have to follow the river to find my bearings. And so, I cut through the mountain in a straight line.

After a good half-day's walk, I reached my destination and found my father sitting on the riverbank. That morning, *Kitci* T8amy had sensed his son's imminent arrival. Through prayer, he had stayed in close communion with me for the entire nine days of the initiation. Like all the great *Okima* of his calibre, his intuition was so sharp that he could stay in contact with people in this way if he wished to.

His only mistake was to assume I'd return by following the river. Consequently, he had his back to me when he heard me approach. Without turning around, his first words were:

"*Kin na, Kapiteotak?* Is that you, Kapiteotak? *Aca na Manto ki pi na?* Have you succeeded in bringing back the Spirit?"

Without uttering a word, I approached him and proudly handed him one of my bear claws. He was prouder than I was in that moment, and hugged me so tightly that I could barely breathe.

"Emma! Emma! *Pican!* Come see who's here and the gift he has for you!"

After the outpouring of joy and tears triggered by this magical reunion, the three of us make our way to my campsite by canoe. We can't leave the Spirit alone in my trap any longer. On our way there, I describe in detail each episode of my impressive duel with *Mak8a*. My parents are captivated, as if they're listening to a radio drama. When we arrive at our destination, we immediately go looking for my bear. He's waiting for us in all his silent might. Dad and I carefully disengage the trap, and it's now Mom's turn to present the Spirit with long prayers of gratitude. She positions herself by his head and places Cedar and water on the ground, speaking to him in the Mami8inni tongue. Afterward, she lingers at several spots all around *Mak8a*'s body, shedding tears now and then for this dear animal and his immense sacrifice.

After several long minutes of prayer, we're ready to open the body. We remove the skin, harvest all the parts that are fit to eat, and meticulously gather the bones. Nothing must be wasted. After such a gift, we never leave anything behind. Once we've completed our task, we return to 8akocik, where the members of the small community celebrate with us and feast on the fresh meat we've brought back. We also save some for later. We'll smoke it and share it with my brothers and sisters, but they'll remain in the dark concerning the real circumstances of the Bear's capture. If they read this book, some of them may remember this happy feast, and will finally learn what we had to hide from them so long ago in the interest of everyone's safety.

Several years after this memorable initiation, I learned that my parents had helped me more than I thought. On the first day, when I found myself alone on the little beach, they hadn't quite left me high and dry. In truth, they hid for over two hours behind the point at the river bend, waiting to see smoke rise from my site. They only set a course for the 8akocik camp after they ascertained that I had indeed gotten to work. Furthermore, my father hadn't picked my initiation site randomly. He had explored the area and found the bear's den. He even felled a few trees nearby, so that I could use them to build a trap. I had noticed that these logs had been chopped down by humans, but I had never guessed that it was a helpful nudge from my dad. My parents had prayed for me and the Bear Spirit for the entire duration of the initiation. I may have had the impression that I had been abandoned, but in reality, quite the opposite was true.

Half a century after my initiation, I unquestionably belong to the Bear Clan. *Mak8a*'s skull sits atop the mound erected in front of my Sweat Lodge—he is its protector. As for his fur, it accompanies me in all my ceremonies. I've lost count of the people who've lain upon it to connect with the Spirit of the Bear, whether for a treatment or for a good night's sleep. Today, *Mak8a* may be losing a bit of hair, for he's travelled quite a bit, but he's ever-present in my work and I still take great delight in telling the incredible story of how we met.

Mik8etc, Manto Mak8a! Thank you for everything!

Sixth Fire

BE PROUD OF WHO YOU ARE

The prophet of the Sixth Fire said:

> "In the time of the Sixth Fire it will be evident that the promise of the Fifth Fire came in a false way. Those deceived by this promise will take their children away from the teachings of the chi'-ah-ya-og' (elders). Grandsons and granddaughters will turn against the elders. In this way the elders will lose their reason for living . . . they will lose their purpose in life. At this time a new sickness will come among the people. The balance of many people will be disturbed. The cup of life will almost be spilled. The cup of life will almost become the cup of grief."

At the time of these predictions, many people scoffed at the prophets. They then had mush-kee-ki'-wi-nun' (medicines) to keep away sickness. They were then healthy and happy as a people. These were the people who chose to stay behind on the great migration of the Anishinabe. These people were the first to have contact with the Light-skinned Race. They would suffer the most.

When the Sixth Fire came to be, the words of the prophet rang true as children were taken away from the teachings of the elders. The boarding school era of "civilizing" Indian children had begun. The Indian language and religion were taken from the children. The people started dying at an early age . . . they had lost their will to live and their purpose in living.

In the confusing times of the Sixth Fire, it is said that a group of visionaries came among the Anishinabe. They gathered all the priests of the Midewiwin Lodge. They told the priests that the Midewiwin Way was in danger of being destroyed. They gathered all the sacred bundles. They gathered all the Wee'-gwas scrolls that recorded the ceremonies. All these things were placed in a hollowed-out log from Ma-none' (the ironwood tree). Men were lowered over a cliff by long ropes. They dug a hole in the cliff and buried the log where no one could find it. Thus the teachings of the elders were hidden out of sight but not out of memory. It was said that when the time came that Indian people could practice their religion without fear that a little boy would dream where the ironwood log full of sacred bundles and scrolls was buried. He would lead his people to the place.

–Edward Benton-Banai, *The Mishomis Book*

It's now my sixth year at Saint-Marc-de-Figuery and I'm fourteen years old. My body has filled out and I've matured. From an Anicinape point of view, I'm already a young man. In any case, considering the realities of the residential school, I had to grow up quickly.

It goes without saying that during those six years, violence was rife inside those walls. It became obvious that we had to do something about it. Many attempted to find help during summer vacations, but no adult wanted to believe us. "How could you speak of missionaries in this way?" our indignant parents would counter. "They are men and women of God. You owe them the utmost respect!" At the beginning, we took some pleasure in defying the missionaries' authority by stealing food or sneaking off during rest periods. Sometimes, we even managed to slip away in the dead of night. We'd play basketball in the yard or visit the young Anicinape women—two of whom were my cousins—who had been hired by the school to help out with cooking and cleaning duties. After dark, we'd climb out the window and scale the chapel cross to reach their rooms. We'd spend many pleasant hours in their company, chatting, smoking cigarettes, and listening to rock and roll on the radio. Then, on the sly, we'd return to our dormitory before daybreak. Naturally, we eventually got caught.

"You spent the night with young defenceless women," declared the Brothers, making a big deal out of it. "You've committed irreparable acts. You raped them!"

That was the first time I heard the word "rape." Of course we'd done no harm to our female cousins and friends, but we could now put a word to what certain Brothers here had put us through over these past several years.

❖

With time, this need to commit such minor misdemeanours grew into a necessity to rebel. Come to think of it, Tommy Wylde may have been the first to incite me not to let myself be pushed around any longer. That day, for the millionth time, we were expected to answer the roll call when they called out our numbers after recess. Tommy had loitered in the schoolyard longer than the others, prompting Brother Boivin to threaten him with a hockey stick. (Now that we were older and stronger, the missionaries had turned to these weapons to hit us with.) This time, however, Tommy had had enough, and in one swift movement, grabbed the stick out of the Brother's hands, broke it on his thigh, and handed the two halves back to the missionary. "Don't ever touch me again!" Tommy had said, looking at Brother Boivin straight in the eye. From that moment on, the missionaries started fearing the older boys. In fact, they had given up sexually abusing us, but they still molested younger children without restraint.

Now convinced that we had to defend ourselves, we'd meet in the woods to plan our courses of action and to toughen our bodies. We had notably taken to hitting trees with our forearms to train ourselves to counter stick strikes. We had also realized that even if we attacked the pedophiles, they wouldn't dare report us to the police, for they truly feared being exposed. With this in mind, we told the younger kids that they shouldn't hesitate to tell us if they were abused. We would protect them.

Alas, if there is one basic rule where pedophilia is concerned, it's that of silence. It's well known that victims of repeated sexual abuse are constantly haunted by fear and shame. Consequently, the children rarely came to us to denounce their aggressors. Even so, there was no need for anything to be spoken outright. The missionaries' degrading actions invariably left their mark on their victims, and as soon as a crime had been committed, we could read it on the youngsters' faces. Whenever we caught sight of a child crying alone, or sitting miserably in a corner eating candy, we would know at once what had transpired. All too often, the wounds the religious pedophiles inflicted were not only psychological, but also physical. Once again, I don't want to go into the details, but understand that our aggressors didn't hold back, and that many children consequently bore the physical trauma associated with rape and sexual abuse. Only one question mattered to us then: "Who did this to you?"

All we needed was a name. Once the children spoke, we could take action. Lunchtime in the dining hall was our preferred moment. The students were all seated at their tables—the boys on one side and the girls on the other. The religious Brothers and Sisters ate nearby but separate from us, inside glassed-in rooms. On denunciation days, a few brave youngsters would anxiously wait for me to stand up during the meal. That was our signal, and as soon as I did, there wouldn't be a moment to lose. We'd run toward one of the two glassed-in rooms to grab the Brother or Sister who had abused a child and drag them into the student dining hall. Some boys would prevent other staff members from intervening, and, in front of everybody, we'd denounce the sick and malicious acts. On a few occasions, we managed to inflict more or less the same treatment on the guilty parties as they had inflicted on us—by tearing their clothes in the great hall or by forcing their heads inside a garbage can we had filled with molasses, sand, and anything else we could get our hands on.

This little scheme went on for some time, but without any significant results. In fact, things were constantly getting worse. The pedophiles didn't seem able to control their vile instincts. By defiling us all those years, they had even transmitted their sickness to some students, who in turn preyed upon their juniors. Other boys now felt the need to fulfill their sexual urges with one another in the woods. In short, we were plunged into utter darkness, and one day I confided to my friends that I was ready to kill, if necessary. What other solution were we left with?

But in reality, I was contemplating another possibility. My suffering had become so unbearable that it had driven me to wish for my own death. And one day, I felt that I was ready to act on it. I managed to escape into the forest with a sturdy rope that I had found in the shop, quite determined to hang myself. However, the deeper I went into the woods, the more my Anicinape spirit recovered its strength, and the less I was seduced by suicidal thoughts. The presence of the trees and the forest's other inhabitants was overwhelming, and my will to live grew once again. I stayed there for a long time, meditating on my fate and convincing myself that I had to hold on—one day, I would get away from this damned school. With a little patience, I would someday finally be able to spread my wings and build a good life for myself. Having gathered sufficient courage, I slowly made my way back to the school. Night had fallen when I reached the grounds and all the doors were bolted shut. "If I can't get back into the school," I thought to myself, "there's only one place left to go—back home to Amos." And so I decided to make my way back home, unconcerned with the distance I'd have to cross, and once I'd get there, I'd explain to my parents that there was absolutely no way I could go on living at the school.

After two nights in the forest and a little more than a day's walk, Amos was in sight. This journey in the forest wasn't very difficult for me—quite the opposite, in fact! I knew how to find my bearings and food, and I found this escapade in nature profoundly satisfying. At some point, I popped out of the woods into a cemetery, where hundreds of Anicinapek and white people were buried. I decided to follow the main road to Amos. Unfortunately, after a few minutes, some policemen who happened by hailed me and made me climb into their car. "What's your name? Where are you headed like this, alone on the road? Do you speak French?" Of course, after six years at the residential school, I knew how to speak the *8emitekoci*'s language, but I chose to stay silent. "I know an Indian lives around here," one officer said. "Let's go to his place first."

The car stopped in front of a shabby old house and the officers escorted me out of the car. They knocked at the door and the man who answered was someone I knew very well: Mr. Hector Polson—my father's very dear friend.

"*Kapiteotak, ati ka ecaian?* Where have you come from?" he asked me in our language.

"I ran away from the residential school," I replied in Anicinape.

Since Mr. Polson didn't speak French and I still refused to answer them in that language, the officers took me to another Indian's house. As we pulled up, a man emerged. To my great surprise, there stood my father! My parents had moved again and I had no idea this was where they lived. I climbed out of the car and rushed into my dad's arms. I tried explaining what had happened to me, but the words came out clumsily and jumbled. In any case, my father was visibly upset and had no interest in taking a compassionate stance. Troubled by my escape and the presence of the police, he remained impassive to my pleas. Although I tried to explain that I'd risk turning violent if I were sent back to the school, my words fell on deaf ears. He cut the argument short with a sharp, resolute command:

"You'll go back to Saint-Marc and you'll finish what you have to finish."

I'm not proud of what happened next, but the fact is that once I was back at school, I blew up at the first opportunity. I lashed out so violently at a Brother who wanted to punish me that Saint-Marc's administrators had me arrested. And this is how I got in trouble with the law.

I'm at the Amos courthouse, waiting silently in a chamber that adjoins the courtroom. The door opens and the judge enters. Someone follows him in, and I'm stunned to see that this person is none other than my father. I don't know whether his presence here should worry me more than the judge's, but I remain stoic. As far as I'm concerned, what's about to happen is just another bump in the steep slope down to Hell. No one had ever come to our rescue before—ever since that damnable day we were first sent to the residential school—and things had progressively gotten worse. Why should today be any different?

"Is this your son?" the judge asks my father.

I would later learn that this magistrate already knew my dad, who had sometimes acted as an interpreter when it came to certain legal issues that concerned our people. The two men had learned to appreciate one another and shared a mutual respect.

"Yes," answers my father. "His name is Dominique. I've been told he's responsible for this whole affair."

"Is this true?" asks the judge, turning to face me. "Are you the one who assaulted Brother Boivin?"

"Yes, it was me."

The judge follows this question with an interrogation that encourages me to speak more and more. For the very first time in six years, someone's listening carefully to what I have to say, and seems to understand the gravity of the abuses we were subjected to inside the walls of the residential school. After listening to my long confession, the judge finally declares:

"Get this boy out of here. I don't ever want to see him at the courthouse or at the Saint-Marc residential school again. From now on, he'll attend public school."

I can't believe my ears. Then, turning to my father, he adds:

"Tom, I want you to stay here with me. You have to make a statement and report this to the police. This has gone on long enough."

Maybe the judge had caught wind of the atrocities committed in our establishment. Maybe there were more adults who were aware of the missionaries' activities than we thought. At any rate, I think that the truth had made its way to Amos and that a few honest citizens had had the courage to listen. Perhaps the judge was merely waiting for the opportunity to intervene.

My father—initially incredulous—began to take in the horror of the situation. Shocked and repentant, he filed a complaint against the missionaries. I don't know exactly what happened next, but after a while, a number of religious Brothers and Sisters left the residential school. From that moment on, lay teachers were hired to take their place, which, it would seem, greatly alleviated the atmosphere within those walls. Still, according to the students, occasional incidents still occured. Moreover, some of the guilty parties were later sent to First Nations reserves by their superiors, where they continued molesting children. They were arrested many years later.

❖

Free! I'm *free*! Flabbergasted, I leave the Amos courthouse. The wind has shifted in my favour. This turn of events—this reversal—is so unexpected! It's as though my prayers have at last been answered! Is it you, *Mino Manito*, who has heard me? Or you, God in Heaven?

When I first set foot in the public school, I'm amazed—I've never seen so many white people of my age in one place. There are even a few Anicinape students here. The days go by and we don't really dare speak to the white kids, even though we know their language well. After all, they're Savages! At least that's what the residential school teachers would have us believe. With time, and especially thanks to the kindness of a few white students, bridges are slowly being built between us. Some of them are frank and curious to get to know who we really are. Unlike the generations that preceded us, ours is no longer condemned to live under the crushing decrees of the authorities. We're the ones who'll start tearing down the taboos.

"So, they tell us you're Savages," the white youngsters quip with a knowing smile.

"Of course not! *You're* the Savages!" we retort, before parroting the nonsense the missionaries inculcated us with.

From then on, our new friends begin initiating us to a world of discovery and possibilities that have thus far been utterly inaccessible to our people. We're in the early 1960s. We're introduced to Ray Charles, The Platters, and Chubby Checker. We're taught the twist and we ride in convertibles through the town streets. Thanks to the younger generations and some open-minded individuals—like Amos's judge—the white gaze is slowly changing. Since 1960, we have the right to vote. Yesterday's prohibitions are being lifted and we're beginning to live slightly freer lives. I can still remember the very first time I was able to enter a snack bar with some friends, around the time I left Saint-Marc's. I had ordered an orange soda for 15 cents. Wedged snuggly in my booth, sipping my soft drink through a straw, I took in every last detail so I could describe the entire experience to my parents.

One day, my older brothers and sisters had wanted to find out what went on inside the local watering holes. My parents, my siblings, and I all crammed into the old car my father had just purchased and we made our way to a bar. Those of age went in, while the rest waited in the car for an hour or two, curious to learn about the establishment and its patrons. My brothers' and sisters' verdict as they left the premises? "They're all crazy in there! They're drinking liquor for fun, but they all end up out of their minds!"

The more the years went by, the more Anicinapek my age wanted to take part in the immense wave of change that was sweeping not only our people, but the entire Western world. My older brothers and sisters eagerly wanted to dress, style their hair, and work like the young white men and women of their own generation. I too wanted to sample this exhilarating social movement, but my parents were intent on keeping me on the straight and narrow path of Traditional Medicine. I remember how, one night, my eldest sister energetically intervened on my behalf: "Why can't you just let him live like everyone else! Give him some breathing room and let him go out a bit!" My parents eventually gave in to the pressure. They let me live my youth like other kids, hoping I would eventually grow bored with this superficial world—that sooner or later, I would yearn once more for the company of Elders.

I dove headlong into the thrilling life of the times, and even became somewhat of a local rock and roll celebrity after my sisters and I started taking part in amateur dancing competitions. With my pointy shoes, tapered pants, and slicked hair, I would send my sisters twirling to the music of Bill Haley, Little Richard, or the great Elvis Presley. We were so agile and dapper that we even became the protégés of the owners of the Club Dragon, an Amos hotspot. They would let us in even though we weren't yet eighteen and take us with them to the neighbouring towns on their dime so that we could compete in all the local competitions. Since we were still minors, the management had concocted an ingenious evacuation plan if ever the police decided to raid the establishment. They had made a wall with beer cases in the huge fridge behind the bar. If ever the police dropped in, all we had to do was to remove two of the cases and crawl inside our hiding place. We'd then simply replace the cases behind us and wait for the bosses to give the all clear when the surprise visit was over. The only drawback was that our fashionable clothes weren't exactly meant to keep us warm, and we would freeze our rear ends off in there!

The intergenerational divide kept getting wider among Anicinapek. People my age wanted to live modern, prosperous, and exciting lives, and were often impatient and intolerant toward their parents, who, they felt, clung too stubbornly to the old traditions. Our parents were powerless against these great social changes, which reached all the way into their homes. In the end, my eldest brother became an airplane pilot, while my sisters—magnificent Anicinape princesses in their day!—all married white men, had beautiful children, and lived in beautiful houses. Unfortunately, a great many Anicinapek, plagued by the memories of residential schools, suffered the ravages of alcohol and drug abuse. Too often, their misery led to suicide.

As for me and my family, we had to cope with my brother Willy's tragic end. He had sunk into the depths of alcoholism and one day was found dead in a ditch. The grim task of identifying his body at the morgue fell to my sister and me. My mother had already left us by then, but this terrible ordeal marked my father for the rest of his days. Losing a child will always rattle a parent to their core. Losing a child who slowly self-destructs until he's found frozen on the side of the road is all the more difficult to bear.

Between the ages of fourteen and eighteen, I too became a loyal friend of the bottle. In fact, I can assert that I made a sizeable contribution to the Molson Brewery's fortune![i] I drank in the hopes of forgetting my problems. After a few years, however, I recognized that I was sinking deeper and deeper into unhappiness as a result of my habit. Eventually, as my parents had hoped, my enthusiasm for dancing, alcohol, and bars eventually petered out. Even though I could easily find all kinds of decently paid jobs and had a bunch of pals to have a good time with, I never felt as though I was completely through with learning what the Elders had to teach me. By the time I reached my thirties, nights out with friends just weren't appealing anymore. That's when I began devoting most of my time to studying Traditional Medicine, all while making my living in fields that were increasingly related to my culture or to my people's well-being.

Before getting there, though, I went through a pretty radical rebellious phase. When I left the residential school, I felt freer than before, but I was far from being rid of my anger. After all those years of being told by the missionaries that Anicinapek were Savages, that they were filthy and uncivilized, after all those years of verbal, physical, and sexual violence, my self-esteem had hit rock bottom. In short, I didn't love myself. And when one doesn't love oneself, one cannot love anything or anyone else. The person who bore the brunt of my frustrations was none other than my poor father. I resented him for having abandoned me at the residential school, and for having taken so long to believe me, even though I had tried to reveal my terrible secrets to him. I resented him for not letting me live my life as I saw fit. I resented him . . . because I needed to resent someone!

My father eventually understood that it was up to him to pull me out of my inner hell. One day, he told me we were leaving on yet another

i An interesting tidbit: the Molson Brewery is Canada's second-oldest company after the Hudson's Bay Company.

expedition. We were headed for the Timmins region, in Ontario, but that's all I knew. I was happy to hit the road with my dad aboard our old Chevy, but I was often impatient—if not insolent—with him. We stopped at a restaurant along the way, and the place was packed full of white people. Everyone inside seemed to eye us from head to toe as we squeezed through to our table. As always, my father paid them little mind. He calmly sat down, ordered our meal in English, and started talking to me in Anicinape—which made me furious. After a few minutes, I couldn't take it anymore:

"Will you *please* speak to me in French when we're in public!" I exploded, clenching my jaw and tightening my fists. "Everyone's looking at us. *You* might not be afraid to be ratted out to the missionaries, but I am. So stop speaking your filthy language!"

My father seemed to get the message and didn't speak another word for the rest of the meal. Then, all of a sudden, he said:

"*Pasik8in!* Get up!"

Thinking it was time to get back on the road, I did, but with a loud and authoritative tone, my father started—again, in Anicinape:

"Take a good look at everyone around you in this restaurant." (At which point everyone turned to see what was going on, but that didn't stop him.) "These people are human beings—your brothers and sisters. You are Anicinape, Kapiteotak. Be proud of who you are!"

That phrase—"Be proud of who you are!"—would remain etched in my memory forever. In voicing them with all the might of the great Medicine Man he was, my father's words struck deep and hit home. I didn't let it show. For the rest of the trip, I kept my mouth shut, doing my best to hide the emotion that this affirmation had triggered inside me. "Be proud of who you are . . ." Had I any other choice but to be who I was? Could I really pretend that I was just like a white person when my dark skin and almond eyes screamed to the contrary? Could I adopt the white language when my heart preferred by far to express itself in the Anicinape language? Could I work in a concrete box in the middle of a city, when all my being was forever calling out for the forest? Could I really appreciate white beliefs, when their men and women of God could inflict so much harm on those they were meant to guide?

❖

Lost in my thoughts, I barely noticed that we had pulled over by a large waterway—the Matakami River. I followed my father, who had climbed out of the car and started unloading our bags. An Anicinape man belonging to the Otcip8e Nation was waiting for us on the bank with a motorboat. My father shook his hand energetically, they exchanged a few jokes, and we then took off on the river, which extended before us as far as the eye could see, carving a winding path through two immense curtains of conifer, beech, and white birch. After a few hours' travel, we reached a tipi village I had never visited before. Several Anicinapek approached the banks as our motor came within earshot. When we pulled in, we were greeted by a handsome grey-haired Grandfather.

"*Mi na ha Kapiteotak apinotcic?*" he asked my father as he looked at me. "Is this the child Kapiteotak?"

My father said I was and the two men embraced warmly. The old man took me by the shoulder and gently led me toward the tipis. Dad and some other men followed behind. I was wary of men who got too close, and I didn't like the fact that this stranger was touching me. Nevertheless, despite my well-honed defensive reflexes, something inside me wanted to trust this old Otcip8e who emitted a great deal of strength and tenderness. Smoke rose from the tipis in the village—a pleasant smell of wood fire hung in the air. Children were playing with their dogs, women and men came and went around the homes, which seemed very cozy and hospitable. We left our bags there, and followed a serpentine trail into the woods until it led to a clearing. At the centre of this glade stood several Sweat Lodges.

We were offered some tea and invited to sit around the fire. Men placed stones into the flames to heat them. Some were depositing Tobacco into the fire and praying in silence. I was about to learn that on this night, the *Matato* was intended especially for me.

❖

Although it's called a "Sweat Lodge" Ceremony in English, this ritual doesn't have much to do with sweating. In our language, we say *Matato*, which could be translated as "Place of the Spirit." Throughout my childhood, I saw my father and the Elders conduct such ceremonies in the utmost secrecy. This particular Ceremony is at the very heart of our spiritual practices.

Our men have been transmitting the teachings of *Matato* for millennia. Admiring how women could experience a natural cleansing of their bodies and spirits every month, Medicine Men asked themselves how they could do the same.[i] And so, the idea of *Matato* took root. They built a hut in a semi-spherical shape and said: "This is the Mother's Womb." They dug a hole in the centre and said: "This is Her Navel." With the dirt they collected from the Navel, they raised a little mound by the hut's entrance, on which they could place their Sacred Bundles. Thus, what was seen within could appear without. Afterward, they lit a Sacred Fire facing the mound, and placed stones into the flames. They said:

"These stones are *kimocominananak acitc kikokominananak*—our Grandfathers and Grandmothers. After they are heated by the Sacred Fire, we will place them into the Navel, in the centre of the Mother's Womb. They will help us commune with all of Creation, our past, our present, and our future. We will pour the Sacred Water over them, which will turn into steam, and thanks to it, we will be cleansed."

Inside *Matato*, there's a perfect darkness—to tame the night and the immaterial. When the hut's door closes behind us, we're at the beginning of all things . . .

For a suffering being, *Matato* is the place of all healing. There, one can laugh, weep, or scream . . . The Grandfathers and Grandmothers can take anything and everything. I was fourteen years of age, and already

i Once, women did not need the *Matato* ritual. Their moon periods, spent in rest and in prayer, was their medicine. These days, due to pollution and stress, their bodies are no longer sufficiently up to the task. This is why we now find women taking part in Sweat Lodge Ceremonies.

collapsing under the weight of many unresolved hardships. Alleviating this burden was urgent. Be that as it may, I had my guard up before entering the Mother's Womb. As the moment drew nearer, the ball of rage that had been growing for years in the pit of my stomach stirred. My nerves were on edge.

"All right. The *mocomak* and *kokomak* are ready," announces the Firekeeper. It's time to begin. I'm told to take a seat at the far end of the hut, in the West. About ten Medicine Men take their places on either side of me, all around the Navel. My father and the old Otcip8e who greeted me are among them. The latter will guide the Ceremony. The first red-hot stones are brought in with a pitchfork, and the door closes. It's very dark—the only thing I can make out is the faint glow of the reddened stones piled into the Navel. A few chants accompany the beating of drums, and we find ourselves deep in silence again. The leader pours some water on the *mocomak* and *kokomak*. *Pssshhh . . . Pssshhh . . .* Every time the water comes into contact with the hot stones, we hear a cloud of steam rise. The microscopic droplets trickle back down onto us, instantly plunging us into an intensely hot sauna. Time would pass very slowly indeed for those who would refuse to enter this symbiotic relationship with the Four Elements—Water, Fire, Earth, and Air. Their heartbeats and breaths would accelerate to the point where, sooner or later, they would simply end up having to leave the Mother's Womb.

On this night, I'm in the presence of experienced Anicinapek, here expressly for me. It's not quite my first *Matato*, but it's the first time I find myself being the centre of attention. I'm tense and my breathing is laboured. *Pssshhh . . . Pssshhh . . .* The Grandfather prays softly as he shakes his rattle and segues into his teachings, drawing them from the Great Medicine Wheel. The whole of Anicinape philosophy—the entire vision—rests upon the circular movement of life, which is marked by the Four Directions—East, South, West, and North. Four colours correspond symbolically to these Directions—Yellow, Red, Black, and White. And four Spirits are also associated with them—the Turtle, the Eagle, the Bear, and the Bison.

The Grandfather stresses most of all the values linked to the Four Directions. In the East, he speaks of life, of everything that's born and born again; he speaks of our own births and of Creation. In the South, his teachings sting a little, for he touches upon self-respect as well as respect for others, which we all too often lack.

The old man speaks in the darkness for a long time, while vapour streams down our bodies. His words are just and true. No one can doubt or contest them. The teachings of the Four Directions carry on for many long minutes, but in this space where one loses sight of earthly references, the notion of time loses its meaning. After each Direction, the leader asks for the door to be opened—an intermission.

Soon we'll broach the teachings of the West. I know that this won't be easy—acceptance and forgiveness will be addressed. In the meantime, water is passed around and we have a few sips. The Grandfather then lies down on the ground by the doorway to rest a bit. The glow of the fire and the full moon trace out his profile. Through the slowly dissipating steam, a blueish light infiltrates the hut. In the distance, we can hear the hoot of *Kokokoho,* the Owl, perched on his branch. The Grandfather slowly rises, and proceeds to light his Sacred Pipe which he shares with us in silence. I observe him in the half-light. His bare-chested and necklaced body radiates the gentle strength of one who's found inner peace. His magnificent silhouette exudes wisdom and power.

The door closes and here we are once again in total darkness. I can hear my blood brothers breathing around me. The old Otcip8e guide thanks the Western ancestors. He softly chants a prayer and, after having showered the stones, he addresses me:

"Kapitoetak, the time has come for you to unburden yourself of your past. Have you ever noticed that all animals on Earth always go forward? Have you ever seen a bird fly backwards? Have you ever seen a fish swimming in reverse? When the Moose steps into the forest, he does not ask himself questions. Despite his imposing antlers and body, he plows straight ahead through the dense vegetation. Nothing can stop him. What is the only being inclined to backtrack and to allow itself to be halted by its past? . . . The human being! Is this the case for you, Kapiteotak? Does your spirit constantly return to the past?"

I have a lump in my throat. "Yes," I manage.

"So, speak, my boy. The floor is yours. The Grandfathers and Grandmothers are giving up their lives for you here tonight. Give them whatever it is that is tormenting your spirit."

Lodged deep within me, my ball of rage makes me suffer atrociously. My breathing is ragged and my heart races. It feels as though if I let but a single sound escape my throat, I'll unleash an extraordinary tempest into the hut—complete with thunderclaps, lightning bolts, and torrential rain.

"What's tormenting your spirit?" the guide asks, louder this time. "Go ahead, Kapiteotak. Headlong, like the Moose. Don't hold back. What did the missionaries do to you?"

This last question—skillfully placed at the crescendo of his speech—reaches into my stomach like a fishhook. The old man went fishing, and, now that he has set the bait, I bite. In one great breath, I spit it all out and my tears start flowing.

"They took everything! My hair, my moccasins, my pride, my language, the forest, my brothers and sisters, my father and my mother. Then they defiled me every day with their words, with their hands, with their eyes. I hate them! I hate them! I hate them!"

And, between two sobs, the biggest question of all surges forth, the great unanswered problem that has tortured every human who has ever grappled with terrible suffering:

"Why? . . . Why?! . . ."

The Medicine Men then commence a chant—a chant of peaceful warriors. They improvise the melody, but their voices are perfectly harmonized, as if they were but one being. Their lament accompanies my cries and sobs. The intensity grows. Their chants encourage me to let everything out. The guide resumes his teachings with renewed vigour:

"The 'whys' kill suffering men. You will never find a meaningful answer to this question if you are hurting. All humans who stubbornly linger on trying to understand why fate has knocked them down are condemned to go around in circles, to lose their way as they search for the semblance of an explanation. White people excel in the art of going in circles in their minds. Meanwhile, the pain remains stuck inside their bodies, their hearts, and their spirits. This pain is what leads you by the nose and makes you erupt at every turn. Your remedy, my boy, is not asking yourself why, but rather to accept what has already happened."

Pssshhh! Pssshhh! The guide pours more water on the Grandfathers and Grandmothers. The temperature rises inside the Mother's Womb and, at the very moment the steam hits the surface of my boiling body, the Grandfather's voice intensifies:

"Accept what happened. You cannot change the past!"

"But how can we keep living alongside all those white people, all those religious men and women who stole our lands and our beliefs? How can one accept to live among these child molesters?"

Pssshhh! Pssshhh!

"Who wronged you, Kapiteotak? Who abused you?"

"The Brothers, the priests, and the Sisters!"

Pssshhh! Pssshhh!

"No! It isn't them. Who abused you, Kapiteotak?"

"The Catholic Church! It's the Catholic Church!"

Pssshhh! Pssshhh! The heat's unbearable. My lungs are burning.

"No! It isn't the Catholic Church!" answers the guide. He repeats his question, more insistent than ever: "Who abused you, Kapiteotak? Who?"

"White people and their government! I hate them! I want them to die!"

Pssshhh! Pssshhh!

"You're mistaken, Kapiteotak."

The old Otcip8e's cadence slows—every word that escapes his mouth is weighed and calculated: "I'll tell you who abused you. It wasn't the Black Robes who hurt you. It wasn't the Catholic Church, the government, nor the white man. The sick man and the sick woman were the ones who violated you, my boy. That's all. The sick man and the sick woman . . ."

These last words leave me panting. I needed to hear them, to reexamine things through this perspective—one I hadn't considered.

Then, the guide cries out: "*Nasema!* Tobacco!" to the Firekeeper who's standing guard outside the hut. As per tradition, he places Tobacco into the Sacred Fire on our behalf. This gesture procures us a form of moral support and helps us stay in communion with the Great Spirit. The Grandfather continues:

"The actions committed by these men and women should never take place—they cause so much pointless suffering. From now on, you will be able to see more clearly into the behaviour of sick humans. However, know this, my boy: when you judge or blame someone, you are poisoning none other than yourself. You move forward through life filled with hate. It isn't good for you. And whenever you come across your human brothers and sisters, your judgments create barriers between you. It isn't good for you, it isn't good for them."

Lying down on the fir branch-covered ground, I let my body weep. My heart's beating fast and hard in my chest, but my spirit has calmed down. I take in my guide's words as he starts again, slowly:

"You're an adult now. You're responsible for your own life. Know how to defend yourself against the enemy if you must, but never pass judgment or blame anyone. It's what wise white men call *forgiveness*."[i]

"Will those who abused me someday seek out my forgiveness?"

"Perhaps they will, perhaps not. Some humans will never really be conscious of the harm they inflict on others. Forgiveness and acceptance will help you free *yourself*, first and foremost. If you do not grant yourself this respect first, no one else will."

The Medicine Man pauses. We can feel that he's said what he had to say as far as the teachings of the West are concerned.

"The time has come to open the door. We must rest before undertaking the teachings of the North. Kapiteotak, will you ask for the door?"

I take a deep breath and shout so that the Doorman outside can hear:

"*Ickotem, cenan!* Door, open!"

i The concept of "forgiveness" does not exist in Anicinape thought or vocabulary. In their outlook toward life and others, Anicinapek prefer to simply talk about respect and acceptance.

The teachings of the North were very gentle. The Grandfather emphasized the importance of knowing how to accept and to let go in order to attain inner freedom. Only then can we truly aspire to true inner peace. The powerful words the old Medicine Man had uttered in the West were reverberating loudly inside me. In fact, I would say they're still reverberating and carrying me today.

I left the Mother's Womb emptied, cleansed, and renewed. The memories of the reprehensible acts I endured or witnessed occasionally came back to haunt me, and I would require many more *Matato* sessions in the years that followed to erase them. Nevertheless, this particular *Matato* proved to be a pivotal event in my life—it oriented me.

It only takes a few words to heal the human soul. One who possesses the intelligence of healing knows how to listen to the wise ones' teachings. Such a person only needs to open the door to their heart, and allow the healing words to work inside their being. In truth, there's nothing we don't already know deep down. Through his speech, the wise man only awakens our own slumbering wisdom.

Seventh Fire

HEALED OF POLITICS, RECONVERTED TO NATURE

The seventh prophet that came to the people long ago was said to be different from the other prophets.

He was young and had a strange light in his eyes. He said:

> "In the time of the Seventh Fire a Osh-ki-bi-ma-di-zeeg' (New People) will emerge. They will retrace their steps to find what was left by the trail. Their steps will take them to the elders who they will ask to guide them on their journey. But many of the elders will have fallen asleep. They will awaken to this new time with nothing to offer. Some of the elders will be silent out of fear. Some of the elders will be silent because no one will ask anything of them. The New People will have to be careful in how they approach the elders. The task of the New People will not be easy.
>
> If the New People will remain strong in their quest, the Waterdrum of the Midewiwin Lodge will again sound its voice. There will be a rebirth of the Anishinabe nation and a rekindling of old flames. The Sacred Fire will again be lit."

—Edward Benton-Banai, *The Mishomis Book*

As I've already said, I never wanted to live on a reserve. Despite feeling unsure about the direction my life would take after leaving the residential school, it was obvious to me that I'd have to work and live freely among white people. I didn't intend on allowing myself to dissolve entirely into their culture, but rather on finding my footing long enough to be able to spread my wings, without being subjected to the geographical and psychological limits of the tiny territories on which the government had parked our people. The powerful *Matato* dedicated to me when I was fourteen had helped me straighten myself out, but pervasive feelings of anger and injustice still lingered. A part of me wanted to move forward, but another part sometimes dragged me back and drove me to drink. And so, I blew off steam by night and worked during the day, where—to my surprise—I found myself enjoying the company of the *8emitekoci* who had hired me.

Sometimes, I was a cook in lumberjack camps. Sometimes, I'd accompany my father in the forest where, on behalf of mining companies, we'd work on surveying jobs and land clearing. The more I gained confidence in the job market, the more I was curious about experimenting with new things. There was so much to learn, so many places to discover and people to meet! Since I wasn't really setting any limits for myself, I even dreamt about becoming a doctor. I confided my aspirations to my mother, and one day, told her the big news:

"Mom, I just got a call from the Amos hospital. They gave me an interview for a new job. I'll be able to become a doctor!"

"But that's not possible, Kapiteotak. You have to study for a long time to become a doctor."

"*Ka8in, Jojo.* No, Mom. I saw a job posting at the hospital the other day. I applied and they picked me. I start tomorrow morning."

At the arranged time, I entered the hospital and proudly announced my arrival. A supervisor asked me to follow her to the basement, where she introduced me to the rest of the team. Everything was going great. Imagine my surprise when the lady handed me a mop and a bucket and gave me my first task—cleaning the floors of the outpatient clinic. *Me!* I'd imagined myself tending to the sick, not having to settle for cleaning chores. But never mind! I'd still be able to see the patients every day and help them in my own way! Besides, I was impressed by my brand new mop and my rolling bucket. They were the epitome of luxury cleaning gear!

I did in fact take pleasure in cleaning the hospital floors to a high shine and making new friends, and meanwhile, I paid close attention to the inner workings of white medicine. One evening, I was diligently doing my job in the radiology room, and found myself in the path of a certain Dr. Chiasson, who was responding to an emergency.

"Will you *please* move!" he snapped. "Can't you see you're in our way? If at least you'd gone to school, you could've done something worthwhile with your life!"

This stinging remark upset me quite a bit, and I shared the unfortunate incident with my colleagues during our coffee break.

"That man judged me! What right does he have to speak to me that way?"

"Bah! You ought to swallow that pill right now, Dominique. That's always how it is with high-ranking types. These big-heads think we're beneath them. If you don't earn as much as they do, you're just a loser in their eyes."

"Well, that's not right. Everybody's important here. I think I ought to speak with Dr. Chiasson."

The next day, I crossed paths with the esteemed Dr. Chiasson once again. He appeared to be less in a rush than the previous evening, so I took the opportunity to have a word with him.

"Doctor Chiasson, I didn't like the way you spoke to me yesterday. You said that I could have done something better with my life. And yet, the patients here need me as much as they need you! I'm here to kill the germs in this hospital. Without my work, you wouldn't be able to do yours. You should recognize that my role is important too. Instead, you passed judgment on me."

Taken aback by my speech and visibly more composed than when we first met, the doctor payed close attention. "Who's this young Indian?" he seemed to ask himself with no little curiosity. He cracked a thin smile at my observations and apologized, explaining that he had been preoccupied with the emergency the day before, and that he regretted his words.

Shortly after, they announced that the then-Minister of Indian Affairs, Jean Chrétien, would be passing through Amos for his electoral campaign. According to my colleagues, the minister would only rub shoulders with the bigwigs, as usual. That gave me an idea.

"So you don't think that we ought to be treated like important people too?" I asked my coworkers. "Well, I have a plan . . ."

All the specialists held titles that ended with "-ist"—so why not us? On the day Jean Chrétien visited Amos, I brought some pins I'd made out of birch bark. I distributed them among a few of my peers and encouraged them to write out their names and their highly respectable title—"Moppologist." It was my good work friend Jean Collin who cleared me a path to the minister. Upon reading my badge—"Dominique Rankin, Moppologist"—the minister instantly took a liking to me and my eminent housekeeping team!

From that moment onward, the work atmosphere and the relations between the hospital departments improved. Dr. Chiasson, who found me affable, now took the time to greet me and to chat a little whenever he had the chance. He even supported my application for a position in the operating room. I would not only be entrusted with cleaning the floors, but also with handling the surgical instruments to get them sterilized. Quite a promotion!

"I told you so," I proudly said to my mother. "I'm climbing the rungs!"

I watched and learned many things in the operating room, but after two years, I felt I was no longer learning anything new. I told Dr. Chiasson I wanted to be transferred to the morgue.

"To the morgue?!" he had exclaimed, astonished. "No one ever wants to work there. Why would you want that job?"

"I'd very much like to see what goes on in there. I know that I'll be able to learn a great deal about the human body and your medicine."

"Well, then, I'll see what I can do. I expect it won't be too hard to get you in."

Dr. Chiasson came through as promised. He secured me a morgue attendant job in no time, and I was notably tasked with preparing the corpses for autopsies. After a few days, intrigued by the disconcerting ease with which I carried out my new duties, Dr. Chiasson and a few other physicians invited me to a restaurant. Sitting before a mouth-watering pizza, I awaited the burning question they had been meaning to ask me for so long:

"You've always known how to keep calm during surgeries and even autopsies. We've never seen anything like it from a newcomer . . . Who are you?"

Without revealing everything (we were barely out of the *Grande Noirceur*), I lifted the veil on my origins a bit:

"My father, my grandfather, and my ancestors were Hereditary Chiefs. This means that they were good leaders, but that they also knew Traditional Medicine. They showed me their way of tending to injured or sick people. Hunters also consulted them to know if their quarries were healthy. Whenever my father had to examine an animal's organs to ensure its meat wasn't tainted, he too performed autopsies. So whatever I've come across in the hospital isn't quite new to me."

That meal, during which the doctors must have asked me a thousand questions—and then some—sealed their fascination with me. From then on, we became great friends. However, I eventually had to concede that my mother had been right—I'd never be able to become a doctor unless I completed some intensive studies. Faced with the fact that school and I had never been a good match, I concluded that I would never become a true "Doctor of Scientific Medicine." In any case, I was sated with the many things I'd seen and learned during my years at the Amos hospital. I was ripe for new challenges.

Despite my short studies, I was often given the opportunity to prove my worth. I was able to learn all kinds of lines of work—postmaster, addictions counsellor, health inspector in Indigenous clinics. I even managed to get myself hired by a small town's police force, although I didn't last more than two months since I found my night patrol duties to be unbearably boring. Still, my stint there opened some doors. I was able to attend the Nicolet Police Institute and undergo training to become a game warden. *That* job was lots of fun! It fit me like a glove. I spent about ten years protecting wildlife in the forests of my native region. I occasionally butted heads with some overzealous superiors, because I didn't like enforcing laws and rules to the letter—indiscriminately and without compassion. I had no desire to police hunters who simply wanted to feed their families. On the other hand, helping dismantle poaching ring operations pleased me to no end. My bosses liked sending me on undercover missions back then. I'd visit the suspected poachers' habitual bar, and simply strike up a conversation. Never did they suspect that the Indian before them was a wildlife conservation officer! All it took was a beer or two for those braggarts to let the cat out of the bag and reveal all their secrets to me. You can imagine their faces when, after the investigation, they'd see me reappear in uniform in time to witness their arrest!

Unfortunately, my conservation career was abruptly cut short. One day we were chasing poachers by snowmobile, and I decided to split from the main group to take a shortcut, unaware that I was headed straight for a ravine. I fell several metres and found myself stuck under my skidoo with a fractured back, unable to move. It took forty-five interminable minutes for my colleagues to find me. They had to helicopter me all the way to the hospital, where a doctor informed me that two of my vertebrae had been shattered.

"I'm afraid you might be paralyzed," the surgeon told me. "If we operate, there's only a ten per cent chance you'll walk again."

"Ten per cent is plenty, Doctor. Operate, and I guarantee you that tomorrow, you'll see me standing on my own two legs."

That's indeed what happened. With a mix of stupefaction and sincere joy, the doctors watched me rise from my hospital bed not twelve hours after the surgery. I took a few steps with all the determination of the Moose, and then . . . I passed out! Still, the battle was won. It left me with a ten-centimetre scar on my lower back—a memento of my hunt for the big bad poachers. The intervertebral discs of my fourth and fifth lumbar vertebrae disappeared and the vertebrae fused. I might be a few centimetres shorter than I once was, but I can walk, lift any object I want to lift, and ride a snowmobile to my heart's content. On the other hand, I regrettably had to bid farewell to my career as a game warden. In light of my accident, my bosses wanted to give me a desk job, but for me, that was out of the question. In any case, Anicinape culture was calling out to me more and more. We had now stepped into the eighties. Openness toward Indigenous people had grown, which allowed for the development of a variety of projects, each more exciting than the last. The time had come for me to put myself at the service of my own people.

When Indian reserves were created at the end of the nineteenth century, Indigenous Peoples were compelled to adopt the white man's democratic system. Those who lead reserves bear the title of Chief, but they're elected by universal suffrage and act more or less in the same capacity as a mayor would. Like a mayor, a Chief has councillors, forming what we call a band council. Every reserve therefore has its Chief, and every Nation has its Grand Chief, an individual who serves as an intermediary between the Nation's reserves and the provincial and federal governments. After those lovely, fun years I spent as a game warden in the forest, and after having had the pleasure of running the Val-d'Or Native Friendship Centre,[i] I was ready to plunge into the world of politics. For a long time now, my father had hoped to see me devote more energy to the well-being of my people and bring my leadership skills to bear. I easily won my elections, first as vice-Grand Chief, and later, as Grand Chief of the Algonquin Nation.

As I entered politics, projects of a social and cultural nature particularly called out to me. I'm especially proud to have played a part in

i Indigenous Friendship Centres offer a multitude of services to First Nations people living outside reserves. In addition to running the Val-d'Or Centre for five years, T8aminik sat on these centres' Boards of Directors—first at the provincial level, and later on nationally—and continues to do so to this day. In 2003, he was named "Senator" for the 140-odd Friendship Centres in Canada, that is, he now acts as an Elder who guides meetings and counsels his juniors.

bringing our language and culture back into our children's education. The elementary schools on our reserves used to reflect the curricula outlined by the Ministry of Education. Teaching Indigenous languages—and even their usage in schools—wasn't allowed by the school boards. After many long negotiations, we were able to get them to agree to the integration of Indigenous languages in students' daily educational programs. This new display of acceptance also allowed us to introduce learning sessions held in the forest, where children could be initiated to skills pertaining to our culture, such as building survival shelters, hunting, trapping, and crafting traditional objects.

Many First Nations communities in Canada no longer speak their respective Indigenous tongues. My people were lucky, for a majority of Mami8inni have retained their dialect. Still, the battle is far from being won. As a result of mixed marriages or relocations to the city, children are gradually losing their language. What saddens me the most is seeing our Elders being left behind. The modern Anicinape lifestyle is becoming as hectic as that of white people. These Anicinapek's day-to-day lives are quite unlike their ancestors', resulting in a rift between young generations and their Elders, the last *Kitci* Anicinapek to be born on the land and to have lived nomadically in the forest. They're extremely precious individuals in my eyes, and unfortunately, very few people give them the recognition they're due. While our youth must work hard to earn their livelihoods (and to overcome the psychological trauma they inherited), the last true Elders are home alone in their rocking chairs. Their presence is sometimes requested in schools, but their inestimable body of knowledge is nevertheless tragically fading away.

I, for one, never stopped visiting Elders. When I worked in our communities, I set up a number of programs to highlight the wealth of knowledge they can pass on to us. With my father's precious and dedicated collaboration, I participated in innumerable museology projects, initiatives to develop and protect ancestral sites, and activities to promote the revival of our traditions.

In short, the years went by and time made a more serious man out of me. I had given up alcohol a long time ago, and I was becoming increasingly appreciative of the legacy our ancestors had left us. I was gaining wisdom—or so I thought!

I did my utmost to serve my people as honestly and as wisely as was possible during my two terms at the head of the Algonquin Nation. And yet, when a system is fundamentally corrupt, there's only so much one man can do about it. In fact, during my years in politics (and still today), money and power sometimes overshadowed the true role of a Chief as it was once understood. And money and power can indeed quickly go to one's head. As I well know! Even though I always acted with integrity when it came to overseeing the funds allotted to my Nation, I must admit that I allowed myself to be seduced by the substantial salary reserved for a Grand Chief. Upon receiving my first paycheque, I nearly fell over—I was making more money than the Prime Minister! At first, I turned the money away. I asked the accountant to redirect a portion to my people, whose poverty is a serious issue. But then, I eventually realized that this sum had never been subtracted from the total figure reserved for the elected officials' salaries. And so, I went back to the bookkeeper.

"You're giving me back my salary in full! And I mean now!" I told him.

My savings account balance skyrocketed. This was new to me. From that day on, I dove headlong into a life of wealth. Obviously, I had to put my fortune to good use! For starters, I bought myself a big car—a Chrysler Fifth Avenue, Special Edition! And then, I also needed off-road vehicles for the forest—a quad for the summers and a snowmobile for the winters. Since I enjoyed retiring to the woods on my days off, owning a cabin seemed like a practical idea. Well, I managed to find one to my liking. Still, it gets chilly in Canada, and it's nice to be able to head down south during the cold season. Everyone was investing in Floridian condos at the time. It was only natural to follow the trend. A condo in Miami! Why not!

To top it all off, I decided to buy a big, 125-horsepower motorboat, which could cross Lake Makamik in minutes. One day, I dropped in on my parents to show them my most recent acquisition, which was sitting proudly on the trailer behind my vehicle.

"See that, Mom?" I said, puffing up my chest. "With that, I'll be able to drive you to your camp in no time at all!"

"I'm afraid not, my poor Kapiteotak," my mother answered, a little discouraged. "That big boat will never be able to reach our camp. The 8akocik River isn't deep enough."

This observation was so on point that it left me speechless. I had gotten carried away by my frenetic spending, and hadn't even taken the time to consider this purchase's real purpose. In her soft voice, my mother then dealt me the final blow:

"What will you be able to see or hear on your big boat? The noise from the engine will scare away the birds and the animals. You won't be able to listen to the silence of nature. Or to take in the beautiful landscapes, which will whiz right by too quickly for you to see! You know, I think I'll stick to my canoe."

There are some who say that the weight of one's set of keys is inversely proportional to one's peace of mind. Well, I had keys to several vehicles and residences, in addition to the weight of my responsibilities as Grand Chief—and the pressure kept rising. My life had grown hectic and agitated, and although I didn't realize it then, my body and spirit couldn't keep up. Things came to a head on one of my many trips between Montreal and Val-d'Or. Not unlike someone who's had too much to drink, I lost control of my Chrysler Fifth Avenue and ended up in a ditch, not far from Mont-Laurier. In light of my symptoms, the police officers who came to my rescue thought I was dead drunk, but it wasn't so. In truth, I was sinking into a diabetic coma.

In today's world, a great number of Indigenous people are struggling with diabetes. The tremendous dietary and psychological upheavals our peoples experienced in such a short amount of time have contributed to the proliferation of this disease. My mother was about to die from it, and now I too was afflicted. I was in a coma for three days. When I came to, the doctor told me I ought to write my will—the chances of me making it were slim. This pronouncement threw me into a fit of anger: "Who does he think he is, talking to me about my own death? No one, besides me, has a say about my fate. If I want to live, I'll live. And that's that!"

They showed me how to give myself insulin injections, and after making some important decisions, I took my leave from the hospital. I had seen that I'd gone too far, and the prospect of death had cleared my head. Like the Eagle, I had climbed high up in the sky, and the path I had to take was clearly revealed to me. I immediately gave in my resignation as Grand Chief of the Algonquin Nation. I sold everything I owned and I even left my native Abitibi. My destination? The Laurentian Forest, where I found an old wooden cabin deep in the woods. After putting up new windows and installing a good wood stove, I spent two years clearing my body and spirit in order to rediscover the way of my ancestors. I built a Sweat Lodge behind my cabin and I often conducted my own *Matato*—alone—no longer afraid to face myself. I quickly saw that my taste for luxury and my long work hours over the last years had subtly replaced my old need for alcohol. I saw that once more, I had sought to lose myself rather than face my old ghosts. I saw that by overworking myself in such a way, I distanced myself from self-respect and self-love.

Once upon a time, my doctor friends in Amos had been curious about me: "Who are you?" they had asked. It was time for me to ask myself the same question: "Who am I?"

"I am Anicinape," I thought. "A Real Man . . . A human being living in harmony with nature." The more I lived in silence, the more time was on my side. The more I took the time to live, the more I could hear the voice of my intuition. The more I listened, the more I knew who I really was. The more I appreciated myself, the more I wanted to be good and true. The more I acted in harmony with my own nature and nature itself, the more

I was in communion with Mother Earth and Creator. The more I made my peace with life, the more my spirit and body felt strong and good.

Once I found this sense of peace again, I felt that my insulin doses had become too strong. I consulted my doctor and, while it was unusual to do so, he agreed to adjust my medication. I stopped injecting insulin and started taking three pills a day. Very slowly and gradually (over several years)—and still under my doctor's supervision—I went down to two pills a day, then one, and finally, I stopped taking medication for my diabetes altogether. By getting back in touch with life and the person I am deep down, I was able to ward off the disease. That said, I'll always have this health problem. In fact, I've occasionally had to take medication to control the condition, but I now know that if I respect my body, my emotions, and my spirit, I can do entirely without. Conventional medicine is stumped by my case, but from the point of view of my people's Traditional Medicine, such improvement is absolutely possible.

Of course, new diseases cannot all be treated with old remedies. And for this reason, I in no way reject scientific medicine. However, I also know that science lacks my people's global understanding of the human being. It's in that regard that our traditional concepts of health can complement those of contemporary physicians. These days in fact, I sometimes receive groups of doctors in my home, and I find the moments we spend together truly pleasant and rewarding.

Cured of diabetes—and of politics!—I decided to move to the Laurentians, that vast realm of forests, lakes, and mountains on ancestral Algonquin land. Doing so also brought me closer to Montreal and the world of white people. My father—who hadn't only become my guide, but my great, inseparable friend—and I felt that the time was right for developing new bonds and relations between Indigenous and non-Indigenous people. The time had come to brush aside the folk image associated with my people and help usher in an era of sharing and dialogue based on the richness of our cultures. The two of us had the idea of creating a small ethnocultural centre, where people could spend a few hours or an entire night in a tipi, sample our traditional meals, and discover our Traditional Knowledge. We found some land and started our company. I was in charge of finding tourists and Dad would tell them our story. Just as our project was about to take off, Dad called me from Amos. A few days before, he'd been taken ill and hospitalized:

"Kapiteotak, I nearly left for good last night," he informed me calmly. "I don't think I have much time left."

"Now, now, Dad. Don't worry about it. I'm sure you'll be just fine. I'm packing my bags and driving to Amos—I'll be with you this afternoon. Wait for me."

I didn't want to take the call seriously. Yet, about ten days before, Dad had asked me to gather my brothers and sisters, without their spouses or children. During this unusual reunion, he'd presented each one of us with miniature canoes he'd crafted out of bark. Most of my brothers and sisters hadn't understood the gesture. It symbolized a great voyage—he was announcing his imminent departure. In fact, he had even said that it would happen two weeks later, and he was right. Like all Medicine Men and Women of his calibre, my father had predicted his death.

On the morning of that final phone call, I had refused to accept the truth. I had only just finished packing my bags when the phone rang again. My sister Jane was on the line to tell me the sad news: Dad was gone. We had known the pain of losing our dear mother ten years earlier, and now, our last pillar had vanished. In the heat of the moment, I was overcome with anger. I couldn't believe it. How could he have left without waiting for me? How could my hero, my teacher, my best friend, my steadfast ally, have abandoned me like this? I was floored. The gaping void left behind by his departure made me realize how dependent I had been on him. My father had been my crutch. I would now have to learn to walk alone.

In truth though, Dad hadn't quite left me to fend for myself. As he'd done in the weeks leading up to my initiation to becoming a young Medicine Man when I was twelve, he had prepared everything ahead of time. After we buried him, I knelt before his headstone, my heart inundated with sorrow. That's when I felt a hand on my shoulder. I turned around to see who was touching me with so much warmth, and I recognized William Commanda, my father's best friend.

"Don't worry, Kapiteotak. I'll be accompanying you on your spiritual journey. Your father asked me to take over after he died, and I agreed. We won't let you down."

Nothing and no one will ever be able to replace *Kitci* T8amy, the Great Man, the great *Okima*. I'll never cease thanking Creator for having had the incredible opportunity to live by this man's side and for everything he passed on to me. Without the exceptional strength my mother and father exhibited throughout their lives, I wouldn't be where I am today. It has been an immense blessing to have been able to receive their teachings, and afterward, those of another great *Okima*, *Comis* William Commanda!

Eighth Fire

THE LIGHT THAT RESTS UPON OUR CHOICES

> "It is at this time that the Light-skinned Race will be given a choice between two roads. If they choose the right road, then the Seventh Fire will light the Eighth and Final Fire–an eternal Fire of peace, love, brotherhood and sisterhood. If the Light-skinned Race makes the wrong choice of roads, then the destruction which they brought with them in coming to this country will come back to them and cause much suffering and death to all the Earth's people."

Traditional Mide people[i] of Ojibway and people from other nations have interpreted the "two roads" that face the Light-skinned Race as the road to technology and road to spiritualism. They feel that the road to technology represents a continuation of the head-long rush to technological development. This is the road that has led modern society to a damaged and seared Earth. Could it be that the road to technology represents a rush to destruction? The road to spirituality represents the slower path that traditional Native people have traveled and are now seeking again. The Earth is not scorched on this trail. The grass is still growing there.

The prophet of the Fourth Fire spoke of a time when "two nations will join to make a mighty nation." He was speaking of the coming of the Light-skinned Race and the face of brotherhood that the Light-skinned brother could be wearing. It is obvious from the history of this country that this was not the face worn by the Light-skinned Race as a whole. That mighty nation spoken of in the Fourth Fire has never been formed.

---

i Medicine Men and Women belonging to the Mitete8in tradition.

If we natural people of the Earth could just wear the face of brotherhood, we might be able to deliver our society from the road to destruction. Could we make the two roads that today represent two clashing world views come together to form that mighty nation? Could a nation be formed that is guided by respect for all living things?

Are we the New People of the Seventh Fire?

–Edward Benton-Banai, *The Mishomis Book*

Dad had left us about five years back. Over the course of my studies and initiations to becoming a Medicine Man, I'd received six Sacred Pipes. One of these Pipes had been presented to me by *Comis* William Commanda, whom I now spent a lot of time with. My last initiation was drawing near. This rigorous trial would prepare me for my seventh and final Fire, that is to say, my final Sacred Pipe.

Was I ready? I certainly thought so. I had been practising the *Matato* ritual and teaching it to those who wanted to learn for forty-odd years now. At first, I had done so in the company of more experienced guides, and later, under remote supervision. My *Matato* had grown considerably in power and heat, for as time went by and I demonstrated my ability, my teachers allowed me to use more and more stones.

I had mastered the Medicine of plants and the Medicine of animals. I trusted in my remedies when I needed them to heal someone. I was also comfortable with the body's focal energy points and knew how to help those whose energy had stiffened or become blocked due to past traumas.

However, the most important thing was mastering the spirit. Humans become sick based on how they deal with the past, hardships, and the very beauty of life. In order for me to accompany others on the path to healing the soul, I needed to possess a good deal of inner personal strength and tranquility first.

When Grandfather William confirmed that it was finally time to prepare for my big initiation, I was thrilled. We got in touch with Medicine Men and Women from Western Canada, and it was ultimately decided that his old friend *Comis* Mikisi, from the Otcip8e Nation, would be the one to accompany me on this very challenging rite of passage, which entailed fasting for twenty-one days on a platform high up in a tree. It wasn't my first platform nor my first fast, but this would be the longest trial of them all.

And so, I set off for the Northwest Territories—just north of the Albertan border—where lived *Comis* Mikisi. He greeted me at the airport. I had visited Elders' homes for private teachings before, and whenever I did, I normally picked up some groceries before dropping in. But this time, considering the nature of my trial, it would have been a fool's errand!

Before heading up to the platform, we spent an entire week preparing my body and spirit. During those critical days, I gradually diminished my food intake. My guide would make me drink the appropriate herbal teas, but above all, he saw to my mental preparation.

"You'll have to remain bare-chested on the platform," he informed me. "You'll have four bison skins to keep you warm. Your body will quickly get used to being denied food, as you must know, but thirst will be a bigger challenge."

"Will I be allowed to drink rain water?"

"Yes, but we don't know if *Kitci Manito* will make the rain fall for you or not. A Medicine Man must learn to submit himself entirely to the will of the Great Spirit. However, there will be another way for you to drink."

"You mean drinking the sap from those big pine cones?"

"The cones will indeed quench your thirst, but mainly they'll provide you with vitamins and minerals. No, the other way you'll be able to keep yourself hydrated is by finding out how to drink the air moisture through the pores of your skin. If you stay well connected to the intelligence of your spirit, you'll manage."

I kept silent—I had no further questions. And then, *Comis* added:

"Don't forget to walk often, up there on your platform. It's very important that you keep your body from getting stiff and cramping up. I'll come and see you regularly. If you get spells of dizziness or if you feel unwell, you must tell me. Don't hide anything from me and don't push yourself too hard. You must learn to know and to respect your own limits when it comes to your body and spirit. Understood?"

"Yes."

❖

We've arrived at the foot of the magnificent hundred-year-old pine tree that'll be my companion for the duration of my trial. The platform was built long ago, in the crook of the strongest branches. Tobacco Ties and bear, beaver, and lynx skulls hang from the far end of the branches. Here and there, Eagle Feathers sway gently in the wind. This is a very powerful place. More Medicine Men have undergone their initiation here than one can count. The energy of our forebears is palpable in the air.

I climb the wooden ladder, which must be at least six or seven metres tall, and set my eyes on the space where I'll be living for the next twenty-one days—nine square metres among the branches. Whenever the wind blows, my perch sways a little. The bison skins are there, as well as a bucket of water for washing. At first, I'll have to go back down every now and then to relieve myself, but before long, these physiological necessities will have ceased altogether.

Comis, who's followed me up, settles in next to me on a bison skin and gives me my final instructions. I take them in attentively, and he leaves me on a final note:

"Above all, don't think about the length of your initiation. If you count the days, you won't make it. One step at a time, Kapiteotak."

The Grandfather leaves and my solitary retreat begins in earnest. It's September. The days are relatively warm, but I suspect the nights will be chilly, especially if it starts to rain. Which it does on the very first night.

Even though I could hide under the bison skins, I shivered all night and barely slept. I thought about the people close to me, about all my loved ones far away and out of reach. I told myself that this trial would drag on forever. I was no longer certain whether I'd be able to get through it.

I'm already in a pitiful state when *Comis* Mikisi comes back the next morning. I'm under so much pressure that it's giving me a headache. I play the tough guy, but he's no fool. He tells me to come closer so he can relieve some of my stress.

"The cleansing begins," he tells me softly as he massages my skull. "We're putting your body through this trial in order to get a reaction out of your spirit. You'll have to confront everything."

He was speaking the truth. During my first week up the old tree, I had to face the cold, the wind, the rain, hunger, thirst, but most of all, my memories. I relived my birth, my happy youth, and the great tear—my residential school experience. Then, I revisited the difficult battle I had subsequently fought in order to keep my head above water and avoid falling from grace.

Whenever the Elder reappeared, my aggressiveness would go up a notch.

His clothes smelled like food, which put me in a foul mood. And he always stayed calm, which irritated me further. I tried keeping my cards close to my chest, but I was contemplating throwing in the towel at any moment. When I finally confessed my thoughts to him, he simply presented me with the facts:

"Either you stay or you go," he stated bluntly. "Make a decision, and then see it through."

Comis was usually so gentle that this sudden firmness struck me. He was right—I had to stop dithering. It was enormously draining. I proceeded to tell him about the visions and nightmares I had had over the last few days. The residential school was haunting me in a powerful way. I had been mistaken in thinking I had successfully cleansed my old wounds, and I now found myself utterly dismayed by how much hold they still had over me. My guide reassured me and explained that I was moulting yet again. He handed me a black cloth bag and said:

"In the coming hours, I want you to place everything that's making your spirit sick into this bag—once and for all. You have to let go of your memories. They belong to the past. You're no longer that little boy who was abused. Your spirit must be free. You see the sun rising over your life every single morning. Your life is ever renewed with every day and every moment."

The following night, a miracle happened. I realized that my wound would always be there, and that sometimes, a word or an action could indeed reopen it. It would fall to me to decide whether I would sink back into self-pity or keep looking forward. "I will no longer be a victim," I decided. "I am no longer a victim!"

For years now, I had taken the time to unburden myself from my sorrow and my anger—and it was a healthy thing. I had to flush out the overflow. But now, I would have to simply *accept* once and for all. Accept everything. The cold, the hunger, the thirst. Accept that the past was over, and that it couldn't be changed. Accept to speak about it freely, with neither shame nor fear. Accept the fact that we all possess within us the power of Medicine, here and now.

I symbolically buried my sickness deep into the cloth bag, and added Tobacco and Sage.

From that moment on, I abandoned myself entirely to the experience. My body found its equilibrium. I was no longer suffering from the cold or from hunger. My wash bucket in the corner was no longer calling out to me: "Come drink." If it rained, I would tilt my head back, open wide, and drink my fill. Otherwise, I made do and quenched my thirst through the pores of my skin.

Grandfather Mikisi was now able to concentrate on the deeper teachings he wished to pass on to me. In the interest of protecting the secrecy of our Medicine and out of a personal wish to keep some of the sacred things that happened to me up there private, I won't disclose the details. Still, I can tell you that the fundamental goal of this initiation involves a great deepening of one's grasp of Medicine—insight on how it acts upon and within oneself. A very powerful Spirit was now in our presence—the Spirit of our ancestors. This presence has never left me.

Sometimes, *Comis* would invite me to lie down on a bison skin and close my eyes. He'd sit behind my head and put me to the test:

"Guess what I'm doing right now."

At the beginning, I felt a little clumsy, but I soon discovered how sharp my senses could be. Since my body was no longer spending energy on exertion, movements, or even digestion, I could devote all my life energy to my presence in this world via my spirit:

"You're taking out your Sage. I can smell it . . . You just laid down your Pipe bowl to your left . . . You're now taking the mouthpiece out of its sheath . . . You just scratched your head . . . You're opening a bag on your right . . . Easy—you just struck a match . . . and now you're lighting your Sacred Pipe."

Sometimes, to teach me to rely on my other senses, including my inner sight, the Elder would blindfold me. I'd sit at the centre of the platform and guess his gestures.

"When you heal people," he would say, "you have to be able to sense all the messages they're sending your way, beyond mere words and the appearance of the physical body. You must put all your senses at their service. If they come to you for help, it's because they can't understand the pain they're feeling. With your active listening and your full attention, they'll be able to enter their own selves and gradually find the path to their own answers. You must learn to enter this space in which you're detached from the outward appearances of disease, suffering, or death. Medicine means staying focused on the spirit's movement more so than the many forms it can take. If you remain tied to your own suffering, how can you possibly help others find the path to healing? A Medicine Man must sense life in motion—in all things, at all times."

The days were flying by and I savoured them to the fullest. In fact, I felt so good that I didn't want to leave anymore. I had lost a lot of weight, of course. If I stuck my finger into my navel, I could feel my spinal cord behind it. No, I'm joking! What *is* true is that I've put all that weight back on—and then some!

One fine morning, *Comis* Mikisi showed up at the platform with another Medicine Man. We exchanged warm hellos, and then my guide handed me a calendar full of pencil marks.

"Count the Xs on the calendar, Kapiteotak."

"One, two, three, four, five . . . nineteen, twenty, twenty-one. Twenty-one days? I finished my twenty-one days?"

I couldn't believe it. With big smiles on their faces, the two Grandfathers nodded and gave me a great big hug. I was so overwhelmed that I burst into tears. Then, *Comis* handed me a cup of fresh water. He might as well have been handing me the Stanley Cup![i]

"Just a little sip," he said. "Taste it."

Well, I don't need to tell you how extraordinarily delicious that sip of water was!

A third Medicine Man soon joined us on the platform. Together, we marked the end of my trial with a long ceremony during which I had the honour of receiving my seventh and last Sacred Pipe. I was also presented with gifts: a magnificent bison skin, Bear Root, Sweetgrass, Sage, and a handful of earth harvested from the foot of my tree. *Comis* Mikisi invited me to place this last gift in the black cloth bag, where I had buried my sickness. We closed the bag for good and purified it with Sage. Then, the Elder asked me to bury it after a month had passed, in a place I would never return to.

When the time came to climb down, the three men wrapped me in a blanket and laid me down on a stretcher they had hoisted up to the platform. They had placed all sorts of medicinal plants on this bed beforehand: Balsam Fir branches, Cedar, Sweetgrass . . . After reclining on my cradle, *Comis* took his place by my side as his two companions lowered the stretcher with cables. They halted my descent on four occasions, during which my guide gave me his teachings on the Four Directions of the Medicine Wheel. Once I was safely on firm ground, the men tied the stretcher behind a horse, and I said my farewells to the tree that had silently accompanied me during my great initiation. After travelling several hundred metres, we reached a big cabin intended for spiritual gatherings. About forty people

i The National Hockey League's most prestigious trophy, awarded annually to the champion team.

awaited me there. We entered and the Medicine Men placed me and my pallet down at the centre of the cabin. *Comis* Mikisi stayed by my side while the people busied themselves around us. There was another ceremony, followed by *makocan*, the celebration feast. Everyone indulged in the great selection of delicious dishes, but I didn't pay much attention because I was completely absorbed by the delicacy that had just been handed to me—a piping-hot cup of moose broth that I savoured ever so carefully.

❖

Within a few days some of my strength had returned, but the celebrations were not yet over. It was time to head south. My entourage of Medicine Men and I drove down to the Yellowknife area, still in Otcip8e territory. Forty-three Grandmothers in a great ceremonial Circle were expecting me when we reached our destination. The warmth of their welcome immediately gave me the impression of being reborn and seeing my mother holding out her arms to embrace me. It was tremendously moving.

The Grandmothers directed me to lie face down on the ground. One by one, they came to me to share their teachings. They spoke to me about respect for life, respect for Earth, respect for women . . . Each of them traced a line on my body with an ochre powder and water mixture. They began with my back, and then asked me to turn over so they could draw on my torso and face. My body was completely red by the time they were done. I was unrecognizable.

There were tipis all around us in this very private place, and in the centre of the Circle burned a great Sacred Fire. Many people came and sat silently behind me to attend the Ceremony. After the Grandmothers' ritual was over, I waited patiently for the next phase—whatever it would be. Suddenly, the ground started to shake. I struggled to understand where this growing vibration was coming from. I could see small trees on the horizon, far to the west. They were getting bigger. Now that I felt I had experienced a rebirth of sorts, it seemed like perhaps Earth was also starting a new life. The trees grew, and kept growing, and then I finally understood what I was seeing—about ten warriors on horseback were galloping toward us, and each held a small Medicine tree pointed to the sky. Every generation was represented, for behind the adults rode children on ponies. All the warriors were converging on me.

One by one, they placed their Medicine trees on the ground all around me, like rays of sunshine.

I heard chanting backed by the beat of drums. The guests took turns touching me, shaking my hand, and congratulating me. I had been admitted to the very private Circle of the forty-nine Medicine Elders in Canada. I was fifty-eight years old—the youngest of the group. The eldest was 112, and his "young" wife . . . 102!

I glowed for a year after that, charged by this great initiation and the extraordinary ceremonies that followed. The power of my ancestors' Medicine has never left my body since—it's always there, in the hollow of my hands. I can feel it. I'm aware of the inestimable gift my predecessors have offered me, and I remain but a small man in the face of it all. I never utilize what's been gifted to me with vanity or to dominate others, nor will I. I'm only inhabited by a deep sense of pride and gratitude.

The Medicine Man in me has truly blossomed. I've learned to draw out from the depths of my being the courage to speak up about the most painful moments of my life, in the firm and sincere belief that doing so can in turn help my peers escape their own silence. I've learned to find the words to convey my ancestors' message of peace as best I can, without fearing the prejudices or taboos of yesterday. I've become a nomad again, and I now travel the world at the invitation of peoples of all nations. Humanity has reached the point where it knows it must put an end to destruction. Humans are troubled by Mother Earth's cries for help: earthquakes, tsunamis, floods, tornadoes, hurricanes, landslides, volcanic eruptions, global warming . . . The signals are multiplying—we can't stick our heads in the sand any longer and ignore the urgency. Could it be that this very urgency is now pushing people to finally give us Anicinapek a voice? In any event, every time I speak in public, I'm touched and amazed to see tears flow and smiles appear on the faces around me when I bring up our Mother Earth, the Great Spirit, life, respect, tolerance, and peace.

Not so long ago, I was still surprised whenever white people gave me the right of way at a crosswalk. We had to submit and reject our heritage to such a degree that I sometimes forget for a second or two that times have changed. Today, I dine with princes and mingle with Nobel Peace Prize laureates. Grandfather William Commanda received many more honours than I, and this kind of recognition always made him smile too. "Back in the day," he once said with a grin, "they called us Savages, and tried making 'proper white children' out of us. These days, I meet a lot of white people who are ashamed of their heritage. Being Indigenous is in. There are even some white people who enjoy dressing like us!"

Comis was touched to see the world finally lending an ear to the voices of our Nation, as am I. Many of our wise ones have gone to sleep, but new generations are awakening. Women are also reclaiming their rightful place after being scorned and trampled upon for centuries. We must heed the distress calls of Mother Earth, but we must also listen to the voice of Woman, who has always kept close to Medicine.

The Four Directions teach us to follow the example of the Turtle and slow down. The Spirit of the Turtle—East—is the Spirit of the Feminine, for the Turtle isn't afraid to enter itself and embrace what comes from within.

In the South, the Eagle teaches us to rise above the fray. The Eagle always draws circles in the sky as he flies. He's showing us how to create our own Circle of Healing, and how to enter it in order to be more present to ourselves.

The Bear, for his part, teaches us to stay strong in the face of hardship. In the West, *Mak8a* spurs us to build our own lives, without fearing the "what will people say"-types and without falling prey to a victim mentality.

Finally—in the North—the Bison helps us see that after having accepted and forgiven (beginning with forgiving oneself!), the soul can heal. Once the spirit is free from its shackles, it can attain tranquility and true peace.

❖

Humans must rediscover their deep bond with nature. The more technologies are within our reach, the more nature pulls away from us. It's the case for the whole of humanity, with its weapons of mass destruction, its polluting power plants, its commercialism, and its media that feeds us more misinformation than truth; but it's also the case for every individual who's unable to slacken the pace, who can't seem to live without electronic devices, or who's forgotten how to nurture healthy and inspiring relationships with others.

Ohiyesa,[i] one of the Dakota Nation's most eloquent representatives during the late nineteenth century, dedicated his life to building bridges between First Nations and white society. At the end of his life, he had concluded that the essential foundations of modern civilization were commerce and trade. He wrote:

> Each man stakes his powers, the product of his labor, his social, political, and religious standing against his neighbor. To gain what? To gain control over his fellow workers, and the results of their labor.
>
> Is there not something worthy of perpetuation in our Indian spirit of democracy, where Earth, our mother, was free to all, and no one sought to impoverish or enslave his neighbor?
>
> Indeed, our contribution to our nation and the world is not to be measured in the material realm. Our greatest contribution has been spiritual and philosophical. Silently, by example only, in wordless patience, we have held stoutly to our native vision of personal faithfulness to duty and devotion to a trust. (Eastman 2001, 62-63)

How many times have I heard white people ask me:

"How can I be at peace with my ancestors, as much as Anicinapek seem to be?" Irrespective of our skin colour, it's undeniable that some of

i Ohiyesa (1848–1929) is also known by the anglicized name Charles Alexander Eastman.

our ancestors caused pain and suffering through their actions or their words at some time.

My people call this the "Teachings of Life." Those people were simply there to show us which road *not* to take.

That said, I'm stunned to see the kinds of history books still being distributed to children around the world. As long as we keep underscoring the wars and conquests of times gone by, we'll keep having a hard time feeling kinship with those who came before us. How can children look to their ancestors for fortitude if their history is chiefly founded on suffering? Now might be a good time to remediate this. If humanity is still alive, still here on Earth, it's because the power of love has always prevailed in the end. If it weren't so, we would no longer be here. That seems obvious to me. Why not focus our teachings on the human race's inner greatness rather than its outward, so-called achievements?

It's also time for us to stop complaining about the fact that the planet and its fauna and flora are in danger, while excluding ourselves from the equation. If humanity suffers, the remainder of Creation suffers. We're all interconnected. Humans are but one link in the chain. Healing Earth and its inhabitants is impossible as long as we refuse to accept that we also belong to this same Circle of Life. We have to go through our own inner healing if we hope to be able to care for others and the planet. You can't have one without the other.

The road to self-knowledge or to our personal spirituality requires time and effort, but the rewards are real. None who follow this path feel the need to look back. Being true, honest, and consistent toward one's values, and expressing one's talents and gifts plainly is much too satisfying to ever regret having chosen this life. Let's not be afraid to devote ourselves patiently to this pursuit. Regardless of individual faith, what truly matters is that a person learns to commune with both their own spirit and the Great Spirit. Only then can one break free of personal difficulties and dance freely on the trail that has been spared from the scorching fires of the modern world. There, the grass still grows.

Our generation may not light the Eighth Fire. That task may fall to our children. Will we have sufficient humility and courage to free ourselves from our ills and from what we must heal together, without necessarily seeing the fruits of our labours with our own eyes? Will we be able to act in the interest of future generations? When I travel to Europe, I'm always struck by the ancient cathedrals looming over the big city skylines. Most of the men who built them never laid eyes on the end result of their hard work, because it often took over a hundred years to complete these churches. Are we capable of the same selfless detachment? Are we capable of laying the foundations of a better world for our children? Of accepting that we are but links in the chain?

What is this Eighth Fire? I invite you to attentively revisit each Fire described in this book. You'll notice that the Prophecy speaks not only of Indigenous Peoples in the Americas. In truth, it includes all humans implicitly, irrespective of their origins. Indeed, the Prophecy alludes to the stages of growth experienced by every individual and every community. We all, one day or another, inevitably leave behind the feeling of being bonded and in harmony with the Mother to engage with the world as it is. Everyone is called upon to face their personal challenges via their own unique and sacred path, in order to triumph in the light of peace. We must all learn to develop our spiritual consciousness in the place where our earthly condition and our celestial reality meet. When we find out for ourselves that life constantly renews itself, when we completely shake off our past or our fears, we become perfectly free. The doors to Infinity are then opened to us.

Death does not exist. The wise men and women of all creeds around the world have never given up saying so. Life is an ongoing, eternal birth. Just look at nature: the flower that wilts on the cherry tree makes way for the fruit; the bear, which feeds on the fish that has only just spawned, will itself leave its body after giving birth to its cubs, and its remains will nourish the earth; in a tiny little seed lies in wait the great oak tree.

Why didn't our Anicinape ancestors ever build temples or statues? Because they preferred admiring the spectacle of life in its constant motion and transformation. How could one possibly illustrate this dance, which is both minute and gigantic all at once? Only the spirit can truly behold the Universe's sacred dance. Capturing and freezing in time an element of this grandiose rebirth (by creating saints, monuments, or even by photographing that which is sacred) is tantamount to illustrating death.

In truth, death only exists in one place—that is to say in the erroneous conceptions of the human brain. It is the human being who no longer knows how to perceive life with the gaze of the spirit, and who, out of fear of disappearing, developed a desire to frenetically control the things around him. Do not fear disappearing. Upon overcoming this fear, you'll find that you're perfectly alive . . . and then, you can never fade away!

The number 8 on its side (∞) is the symbol for Infinity. The Eighth Fire invites us to find Infinity. Strangely, those who gave the Algonquins a written language included "8" in our alphabet. A fitting coincidence, don't you think?

Let us become free again and touch the Infinite. This is what my ancestors have taught me. That is what it is to be Anicinape. Everyone can become Real again and live in harmony with nature. Let us be free like the animals in the wild—without apprehension for tomorrow, without the weight of our past, without worrying about fading away. Most importantly, let us be proud to be human. We received an inestimable gift that animals did not—Consciousness. Let us celebrate it!

Acknowledgments

A big *mik8etc* to all those who helped make this book a reality:

Mik8etc to my parents, Emma and T8amy, who gave me everything.

Mik8etc to the late *Comis* William Commanda, for his precious teachings and the privilege of having been able to learn at his side for so long.

Mik8etc to Edward Benton-Banai, for his permission to use his text of the Prophecy of the Seven Fires. Mr. Benton-Banai is an Elder from the Otcip8e Nation and Grand Chief of the Three Fires Mitete8in Lodge in Wisconsin. The Prophecy, as it was revealed to him in a series of visions, can be read in full in *The Mishomis Book: The Voice of the Ojibway.*

Mik8etc to the Secrétariat aux affaires autochtones in Quebec City, and particularly former Deputy Minister André Maltais for his precious help in the realization of this project.

Mik8etc to Elders Anne, Albert, and Fred Mowatt of Pikogan, who witnessed my birth and related to me in detail the circumstances surrounding the airplane accident. It is always a great pleasure to visit with you.

Mik8etc to my sisters Cécile, Hélène, Jane, and Marie, as well as my brother Léo, for their memories of our childhood, when mine were hazy.

Mik8etc to our publisher Joanne Therrien at Vidacom Publications, for making it possible to share this story with an English audience. To editor and translator Ben Vrignon, as well as Lynne Therrien and the rest of the team, for their remarkable work and delicate, respectful handling of our traditions and culture. And also to graphic designer Charity Webster of Relish New Brand Experience, for bringing all the elements of this project into the elegant book you now hold in your hands.

Mik8etc to Les Éditions Le Jour for their marvelous work on *On nous appelait les Sauvages*, the original French edition of this book. To Linda Nantel, who believed in our project from the very beginning. To publisher Erwan Leseul, for his enthusiastic and warm welcome in the early years of the project. To the graphic design and PR team (a special *mik8etc* to the two Roxanes!) for their creativity and their heartfelt dedication.

Mik8etc to our late friend Nancy Lessard, who, with her assistant Maxime Boisvert, captured the magnificent portrait featured on the cover of this book. It is one of the last photographs Nancy took before we lost her to cancer.

Finally, *mik8etc* to *Kokom* Marie-Josée, who, thanks to her wonderful listening skills and writing talent, was able to find the words to express what my heart wished to share with you.

Works Cited

Benton-Banai, Edward. 2010. *The Mishomis Book: The Voice of the Ojibway.* Minneapolis: University of Minnesota Press.

Eastman, Charles Alexander. 2001. *The Soul of an Indian: And Other Writings from Ohiyesa.* Edited by Kent Nerburn. Novato: New World Library.

Eastman, Charles Alexander. 2007. *The Essential Charles Eastman (Ohiyesa): Light on the Indian World.* Edited by Michael Oren Fitzgerald. Bloomington: World Wisdom.

Le Clercq, Chrestien. 1910. *New Relation of Gaspesia: With the Customs and Religion of the Gaspesian Indians.* Translated and edited by William F. Ganong. Toronto: The Champlain Society.

National Archives of Canada, Record Group 10. 1920. vol. 6810, file 470-2-3, vol. 7, 55 (L-3) and 63 (N-3).

Stone, William L. 1851. *Life of Joseph Brant—Thayendanegea: Including the Indian Wars of the American Revolution. Vol. II.* New York: Phinney & Co.

About the Authors

T8aminik Rankin and Marie-Josée Tardif have devoted their lives to preserving and passing on Indigenous culture and heritage. For many years now, they have been sharing their teachings and wisdom with Indigenous and non-Indigenous people alike—across Canada and abroad—through educational projects, public ceremonies, conferences, intervention programs, and spiritual healing workshops. Together, they cofounded the non-profit organization Kina8at, and more recently, the Dominique Rankin Foundation. Established to help Indigenous Peoples heal and reconnect with their roots, these initiatives also promote Indigenous culture and heritage at large, in the spirit of joy, respect for Mother Earth, and reconciliation.

To learn more about the authors and their latest projects, please visit their websites:

www.dominiquerankin.ca | www.mariejoseetardif.ca
www.kina8at.ca
www.dominiquerankinfoundation.com